I Is for Infidel

I Is for Infidel

FROM HOLY WAR
TO HOLY TERROR:
18 YEARS INSIDE
AFGHANISTAN

Kathy Gannon

PublicAffairs

New York

BOOK DESIGN AND COMPOSITION BY JENNY DOSSIN.

Library of Congress Cataloging-in-Publication Data
Gannon, Kathy.
I is for infidel: from holy war to holy terror: 18 years inside Afghanistan /
Kathy Gannon.—1st ed.
p. cm.
Includes index.
ISBN-13 978-1-58648-312-8
ISBN-10 1-58648-312-9
1. Afghanistan—History—Soviet Occupation, 1979–1989.
2. Afghanistan—History—1989–2001.
3. Afghanistan—History—2001–. I. Title.
DS371.2.G365 2005
958.104'5—dc22
2005048667

FIRST EDITION

1 3 5 7 9 10 8 6 4 2

To my mother and my sister for their love

To the memory of my friend Kathy Evans

To my husband, Pasha,
who is the most wondrous of dreamers,
and who reminds me every day of
the possibilities of tomorrow

CONTENTS

	Map of Afghanistan	*viii*
	Cast of Characters	*ix*
	List of Photographs	*xi*
PROLOGUE	Friends or Foes	*xiii*
CHAPTER ONE	The Way It Was	*1*
CHAPTER TWO	Inside the Taliban	*21*
CHAPTER THREE	The Beginning of the End	*37*
CHAPTER FOUR	The Moderate Taliban	*51*
CHAPTER FIVE	The Taliban Bloodied	*67*
CHAPTER SIX	The Last Days of the Taliban	*83*
CHAPTER SEVEN	After the Taliban	*109*
CHAPTER EIGHT	The Hidden Face of Pakistan's Military	*127*
CHAPTER NINE	Ties That Bind	*149*
EPILOGUE	Four Years Later	*165*
	Acknowledgments	*175*
	Index	*179*

MAP OF AFGHANISTAN

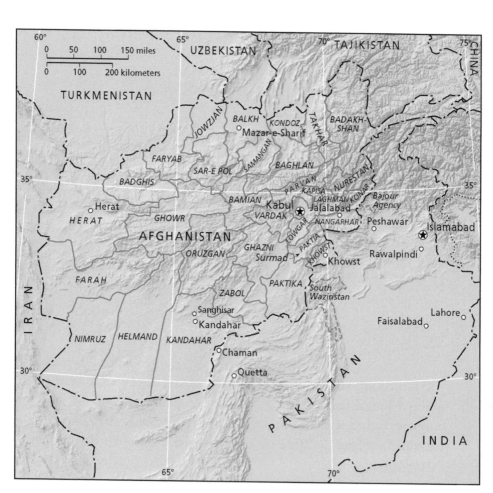

Map courtesy of Bowring Cartographic

Mujahedeen (Warlord) Government 1992–6
(Supported by U.S.)

RASHID DOSTUM: allied first with communist, then with Massood, and then with Hekmatyar

MOHAMMED FAHIM: interior minister who ordered Karzai arrested

JALALUDDIN HAQQANI: key commander in mujahedeen government

GULBUDDIN HEKMATYAR: prime minister who attacked Kabul for four years

HAMID KARZAI: deputy foreign minister

MAULVI YOUNIS KHALIS: education minister who dismissed education for girls as unnecessary, welcomed Osama bin Laden to Afghanistan from Sudan

AHMED SHAH MASSOOD: defense minister and ethnic Tajik who ignored Karzai requests to bring ethnic Pashtuns into the government and to Kabul from the south and the east of the country, killed on Sept. 9, 2001 by Tunisian suicide bombers posing as television journalists

ABDUL RASUL SAYYAF: factional leader who controlled interior ministry, whose soldiers committed atrocities, operated training camps and welcomed Osama bin Laden to Afghanistan from Sudan

GUL AGA SHERZAI: governor of southern Kandahar province, warlord, and drug baron

HAJJI ABDUL QADIR: governor of eastern Nangarhar province who gave welcoming speech at lunch for Osama bin Laden after he arrived in Afghanistan from Sudan in 1996

Taliban Government 1996–2001

QATRADULLAH JAMAL: information minister

JALALUDDIN HAQQANI: key commander in Taliban government

MULLAH MOHAMMED KHAKSAR: moderate Taliban, former intelligence minister, still in Kabul

MULLAH WAKIL AHMED MUTTAWAKIL: former foreign minister, moderate

MULLAH OBEIDULLAH: defense minister

MULLAH MOHAMMED OMAR: fought in U.S.-backed war against invading Soviet Union, founded Taliban to end lawlessness of mujahedeen, imposed repressive and rigid interpretation of Islam

President Hamid Karzai's Government December 2001– (Supported by the U.S.)

MOHAMMED FAHIM: former defense minister

HAMID KARZAI: president

MAULVI YOUNIS KHALIS: allied to Qadir's provincial government

HAJJI ABDUL QADIR: governor of eastern Nangarhar province and Cabinet minister until his death in 2002

ABDUL RASUL SAYYAF: key advisor

GUL AGA SHERZAI: Kandahar governor (briefly Cabinet minister)

LIST OF PHOTOGRAPHS

*All photos are courtesy of the *Associated Press*, unless otherwise indicated.

Page 1   Top—Gulbuddin Hekmatyar with Commander Jalaluddin Haqqani in Jalalabad, Afghanistan. Photo courtesy of Bangash Khan.
Middle—Hekmatyar reviews guard of honor in Islamabad, Pakistan. Photo courtesy of Bangash Khan.
Bottom—Hekmatyar is sworn in as prime minister of Afghanistan in 1996 by Burhanuddin Rabbani (left). Looking on is Abdul Rasul Sayyaf (right).

Page 2   Top—Author Kathy Gannon at Torkham border post in 2001 with Riaz Khan (center) and Mullah Hanifi (right).
Bottom—U.S. leaflets dropped throughout the countryside to persuade Afghans to help against the Taliban.

Page 3   Top—Former Afghan communist president Najibullah and his brother are hung in the Kabul town square.
Bottom—Taliban members celebrate Afghan independence in Kabul, less than two months before the 9/11 attacks.

Page 4   Taliban escort Christian missionaries back to their cells.

Page 5   Setting up a satellite telephone on the border of Afghanistan and Pakistan.

Page 6   Mullah Mohammed Khaksar, former Taliban intelligence chief

Page 7   Destroyed Bamiyan Buddha

Page 8   Abdul Rasul Sayyaf addresses a news conference with Ahmed Shah Masood. Photo courtesy of Bangash Khan.

Friends or Foes

Karim is not his real name. I know my friend's real name, but he is too afraid to use it.

Fear, war, and repression are like threads woven into the fabric of Afghans: fear of the Russians, of the mujahedeen, of the Arabs, of al Qaeda, Pakistanis, Americans, B-52 bombers, and of each other.

My friend is a man with a history. His left arm is slightly disfigured, the elbow smashed by a Russian bullet, a battlefield scar gained fighting the invading Soviet soldiers in the 1980s. Back then, he was a brave mujahedeen, unmoved by the sight of the Russian enemy, unafraid to heave a rocket launcher onto his shoulder, take aim, and fire. But in 2004 near the border of Afghanistan, as he sits across from me, he is too afraid to be identified.

"Do you want me to be killed?" His smile is nervous. He doesn't say anything else. He just looks at me, silently. I wonder what to do.

We're sitting at a long wooden table that is hidden beneath a coffee-stained tablecloth at a hotel in Pakistan's frontier city of Peshawar, not too far from the border with Afghanistan. It's a rugged little city largely inhabited by fierce Pathan tribesmen, who live on both sides of the border, here and in Afghanistan.

Peshawar is about 400 kilometers from the Afghan capital of Kabul and relatively safe for my Afghan friend. I've always loved Peshawar. There is a romance about the city, which looks eastward to the Khyber Pass, a historically treacherous stretch of road that nineteenth-century British colonialists could neither tame nor travel without being massacred. Peshawar sits at the crossroads of the ancient silk route. In its heart, snuggled in the middle of aromatic spice bazaars, where everyone is deafened by a cacophony of screaming rickshaws and blaring car horns, is the storyteller bazaar. Its name harkens back some 2,000 years to a time when caravans of weary traders, their animals bundled high with exotic silks and spices, would stop for the night, bed their tired beasts, and trade stories of the road they had just traveled and the dangers they had faced.

The first time I visited Peshawar was in 1986. Then, nearly 5 million Afghans, who had fled a Soviet invasion of their homeland, lived as refugees in camps that crowded in on Peshawar.

A lot has happened in the intervening years. The Soviet Union withdrew its occupation troops and a brutal civil war among Islamic mujahedeen groups followed; their feuding ways gave rise to the repressive Taliban regime, which was cut down by the U.S.-led war in 2001, bringing in Hamid Karzai's government and returning many of the same feuding mujahedeen to positions of power. So much has changed, yet so little has changed.

I look down at the tablecloth, finger the teaspoon, wait for my friend to say something. I pour another cup of coffee. It's cold now, and the milk, which had been boiled, has coagulated. There's a television on in the corner of the room. The picture is fuzzy, but it's easy to see it is a cricket match, a popular sport in this part of the world.

Finally, my friend decides. He doesn't look directly at me and I don't try to make eye contact. I can feel his nervousness, and that he is ashamed of his fearfulness. When at last he speaks, his head is slightly bowed.

"Please, my friend, don't say who I am."

I agree, and that's when we decide to call him Karim.

Karim isn't much older than thirty-eight. An ethnic Pashtun from Afghanistan's eastern Nangarhar Province, of which Jalalabad is the capital, he's fluent in Arabic, weak in English, but improving every day. His face is handsome, with deep brown almond-shaped eyes and a neatly trimmed black beard. He studied Arabic in Peshawar at the Institute of Imam Abu Hanifa, which is funded, he tells me, by Saudi Arabia and Kuwait.

I understand his fear. The topic of our conversation is a dangerous one. Karim was in Jalalabad in May 1996 when Osama bin Laden arrived from Sudan. He knows the details of his arrival, details that implicate powerful men in today's Afghanistan, men who sit with Afghan president Hamid Karzai, who are welcomed at the heavily fortified U.S. Embassy in Kabul to meet the U.S. ambassador in Afghanistan. These men were returned to positions of power by the United States and its coalition partners in 2001, men like Abdul Rasul Sayyaf.

One August day in 2004, when I was having breakfast with Hamid Karzai on the lush green lawns of the presidential palace in Kabul, he described Sayyaf as an ideologue in a way that sounded complimentary. But Sayyaf is a vicious man, whose followers have carried out unspeakable atrocities and horrific massacres of Afghanistan's ethnic Hazaras.

Abdul Rasul Sayyaf inspires violence in others: Abu Sayyaf, a Philippine terrorist organization, was named for him by its founder, Abdurajak Janjalani. Janjalani was a disciple and a student of Sayyaf's who received military training from him. The Indonesian Mohammed Nasir Bin Abbas, alias Solaiman, who was arrested in Indonesia in April 2003, was trained under Sayyaf between 1987 and 1991. Bin Abbas used the terrorist training he received from Sayyaf to set up Camp Hodeibia in the Philippines, according to Maria Ressa's account in *Seeds of Terror* (New York: 2003). This camp was later taken over by Umar Patek, an Indonesian who has been implicated in the 2002 bombing on the resort island of Bali in which more than 200 people were killed.

A report put together from information collected by more than one Western intelligence agency and revealed by the newspaper *Al Watan Al Arabi* tells of a particularly terrifying meeting held soon after bin Laden's arrival in Afghanistan, before the Taliban took power and while Sayyaf and his mujahedeen colleagues were ruling the country. My friend Karim had also heard the details of the meeting, although he hadn't been present at it.

It was convened in northwest Pakistan's remotest tribal regions, tucked away on an arid plateau surrounded by hills and guarded by hundreds of men hidden in the trees and crevices of the mountainside.

The high-level secret meeting brought together some of the most radical of groups and nations, who accused the West then in 1996, a full five years before the September 11 attacks, of waging a war against Islam. The participants urged a counteroffensive and spoke of attacking the United States and the West. They spoke of their hatred for the West and their revulsion for governments in the Middle East that sympathized with the West.

Fundamentalist organizations in Egypt, Yemen, Iran, and other Gulf states were represented, as were militant groups from Pakistan, Algeria and Sudan. They sat beside dissidents who lived in London, Tehran, and Beirut. They had come together to plot a war against American and Western interests.

Convinced that the West had already begun a war against Muslims, they wanted to retaliate, go on the offensive, and take the battle to the enemy on their own terms. This was not their first gathering. There had been at least one earlier meeting in Iran to lay the ground for this gathering, to settle religious and ideological differences that would allow these men to come together to wage a single war against a single enemy—the West.

And so a huge tent was pitched on the high plateau, under the watchful guard of the sentries in the ring of hills. A noisy generator provided light. Ghostly shadows were visible from outside, backlit against the walls of the tent as the participants moved inside. It was an eerie sight.

Men arrived in four-wheel-drive vehicles that had rumbled up the tortuous roads. The first to arrive was Osama bin Laden's lieutenant, Aymen al-Zawahri. The conversation focused on Benjamin Netanyahu's rise to power in Israel. One man, who seemed to have come from a European country, spoke of a vicious offensive being readied against Islam.

The men talked for another two hours until Osama bin Laden joined the gathering. At his side was Abdul Rasul Sayyaf. It was Sayyaf who spoke first. Bin Laden listened. Sayyaf shared bin Laden's revulsion for U.S. troops in Saudi Arabia. He praised the violent bombing one month earlier in al-Khubar in Saudi Arabia that had killed more than twenty U.S. servicemen, for which al Qaeda had been held responsible. Sayyaf's small brown eyes seemed to glow as he recounted the bombing. He reveled in the description of it, saying it should be a lesson to America to withdraw its troops from Saudi Arabia. He likened it to the 1981 and 1983 bombings in Beirut of the U.S. Embassy and its military compound that had killed hundreds of U.S. soldiers and led to the American withdrawal from Lebanon.

Sayyaf's speech inspired an Iranian to call for an all-out offensive against America. He was frenzied. He warned that the Muslim world was facing its gravest conspiracy. It wasn't clear whether he had been sent by the government or whether he represented a jihadi group. Another speaker joined in, this time from Bahrain. His words were angry, his voice rising as he spoke: "We are enduring coercion and humiliation in our own country." Then an Egyptian spoke. He castigated his own government for spurning an offer from Syria to mediate its differences with Iran.

The men talked into the night. As dawn broke, a man from London looked to Sayyaf for direction. What should they do? What strategy should be adopted?

Sayyaf's voice was low. "Let us wait until this evening, when we resume our discussions. I will then speak and give my opinion as one who believes in what you believe and who is ready to fight in the same trench as you."

When they reconvened, it was brief, the decision firm. They would confront the United States and the West. The organizations represented at the meeting would work together, they would devise strategies, plots, coordinate. In this way, in mid-1996, high in the lawless tribal lands of northern Pakistan, the terrorist networking began.

After the meeting, Sayyaf returned to Kabul to resume his role in the mujahedeen-led government of Afghanistan, a government that owed its existence to the support it had received from America.

⧉

As I sat across from Karim in the noisy hotel coffee shop in Peshawar, I began fully to understand his fear. Sayyaf's men had been among those who had welcomed bin Laden to Afghanistan in 1996, along with others from that mujahedeen government who had also been returned to power by the United States in 2001. These same men had encouraged and allowed terrorist training camps when they were in power from 1992 until 1996. They had lied to the CIA in September 1996 when the agency had requested their help in finding bin Laden. The CIA's intelligence was so flawed that it wrongly said that the Taliban brought bin Laden to Afghanistan in 1996 and that the Taliban's leader, Mullah Mohammed Omar, knew bin Laden before he came to Afghanistan in 1996. He didn't. It was Abdul Sayyaf, America's "ally," who had welcomed bin Laden.

My friend Karim didn't see the United States and the West as a source of comfort or protection. He fidgeted with his beard. His voice broke. His usual speaking voice is a baritone, but when he gets excited or worried it rises and cracks, becoming squeaky sounding.

I worried for him. He knew who had been present at a series of April 1996 clandestine meetings among the mujahedeen, meetings held in lantern-lit rooms to discuss giving bin Laden sanctuary in Afghanistan. Then Sudan, under relentless pressure from the United States, wanted bin Laden gone.

A friend of Karim's went to Khartoum to meet bin Laden. Karim's voice dropped to barely a whisper as he recalled the conversations. I strained to listen.

> My friend met Osama. Osama had a question. He said to my friend: "I have more problems with America and the problems that Sudan has today with America; maybe tomorrow Afghanistan will have these problems and what will your reaction be?" My friend didn't have an answer for him. He had to return to Jalalabad and ask the mujahedeen.
>
> The mujahedeen knew that America wanted Osama, but they didn't mind. They called a *shura* [council meeting of elders] and the *shura* gave its decision: "Afghanistan has had twenty years of war. It has been destroyed by all these wars and fighting. We have thousands of problems and if Osama is one more problem, what is that? He is a Muslim. We should help. What are problems for Afghans? God will solve all our problems. Tell him to come."

Among the key figures at the *shura* that April day in 1996 were lieutenants of Sayyaf and of other mujahedeen leaders, who today hold positions of power in Afghanistan.

CHAPTER ONE

The Way It Was

It was a crisp cool morning on September 26, 1996, when I returned to Afghanistan on a Red Cross flight from Pakistan. The fractious mujahedeen government was under siege by the Taliban, who were closing in on Kabul. I wanted to see just how close they had gotten.

I stepped down the narrow stairs of the aircraft, clinging to the rope handles to balance myself. The tarmac was crowded with international aid workers waiting to board, to get out of Afghanistan before the Taliban entered the city. They said the city could be overrun within hours. I thought it would be days, maybe even weeks.

I had assumed that this would be one of many trips I would make to Afghanistan before the Taliban were in a position to overthrow the mujahedeen government, which was made up of the guerrilla factions that had forced the withdrawal of invading Soviet soldiers in 1989 and the collapse of Afghanistan's Communist government three years later in 1992.

The mujahedeen's four years of rule had been one long bloody war between rival factions within the government, which was dominated by the Northern Alliance. By 1996, Kabul was in ruins, buildings were crumpled heaps of stone, brick, and cement.

An Afghan Red Cross worker told me she said good-bye to her husband and young son each morning, never sure they would be alive when she returned. Each time she heard the thud of an incoming rocket, her heart sank and she whispered a prayer: "Please, God, please keep my family safe."

On that afternoon of September 26, events moved much quicker than I had anticipated. It turned out that the Red Cross aircraft that dropped me off would be the last plane in or out of Kabul for the next ten days, as the Taliban seized control.

Rockets could be heard from a distance, but still I thought the mujahedeen government was in control of the city. Their collapse didn't seem imminent and I went looking for someone to talk to, perhaps from the Afghan Foreign Ministry or from the Defense Ministry. I found Dr. Abdullah, sometimes referred to as Abdullah Abdullah. He has always seemed more diplomat than warrior, although he has spent all his time at the side of Ahmed Shah Massood, the first post-Communist defense minister. Abdullah has the uncanny ability of knowing and saying what foreigners want to hear, regardless of whether it's true. He would later become the first foreign minister in Hamid Karzai's government. But that afternoon he was a mujahedeen spokesman and in a defiant mood.

He insisted that the mujahedeen fighters would not be defeated. His exact words were: "We will fight until our last drop of blood." I should have known then that their defeat was imminent because in Afghanistan that promise was generally made just before a hasty retreat.

After so many years covering Afghanistan, I now understand what Afghan leaders really mean when they talk about shedding the last drop of blood. They certainly don't mean their own. It is usually the blood of innocent civilians caught in the cross fire. When leaders' lives are threatened, their first inclination is to beat a hasty retreat.

That day in Kabul, behind his angry bluster, Dr. Abdullah was getting ready to run. He railed against Pakistan for supporting the Taliban and against the United States, accusing America of propping up the Taliban. Westerners were not popular that day in Kabul.

I discovered just how unpopular we were when I headed toward the front lines. On the way to Pul-e-Charkhi, a small village on the eastern outskirts of Kabul where the country's biggest and most notorious prison was located, I heard not only the thud of incoming rockets but the nearby stammer of small-arms fire. It was getting louder and yet we were still far from Pul-e-Charkhi. At first I couldn't figure out what was going on. The incoming rockets were getting closer, too close if the mujahedeen government was going to be able to hold on to power.

Several Northern Alliance soldiers caught sight of our car and the foreigners within. They were angry, very angry. One young soldier grabbed his Kalashnikov rifle and began pounding its butt on the hood of our car. His face was contorted with fury, his eyes blazing with anger, his rage directed at us. I didn't understand why.

I asked Abdullah Zaheeruddin, the Associated Press correspondent in Kabul at the time, to stop the car so we could talk to the soldier. I am sure he thought I was crazy, but he did. The soldier screamed something at us in Persian. All I could make out from his ranting was "America," and it didn't sound flattering. Abdullah translated: "Go home to America. It is America who brought the Taliban."

We tried to move closer to the fighting, inching our way toward Pul-e-Charkhi. We hadn't yet reached the outskirts of the city, but we couldn't go any further. Within moments, still well within Kabul, we found the front lines. Rockets blasted in toward us from the Taliban side. Behind us, the Northern Alliance soldiers continued to brandish their Kalashnikovs at us, screaming for us to get out, go home, leave.

We did, and quickly, returning to the city center, barely three kilometers away, where some Northern Alliance officials could be found who were still not ready to concede defeat, promising, like

Dr. Abdullah, to fight on until the last drop of their blood, or as it turned out, until later that night when they slipped out of Kabul under the cover of darkness. Kabul, and with it Afghanistan, had been abandoned to the Taliban.

I was at the only United Nations guest house that night, one of the rare places in Kabul where you could get a drink. The bar was stocked with alcohol retrieved from a hidden storage compartment in the U.S. Embassy, which had been closed for more than a decade.

As I sipped a whiskey, I wondered what was happening to Afghanistan's former Communist president Najibullah, who was living under house arrest just a few blocks away in a UN compound. He had been there since 1992, forced to seek UN protection when the mujahedeen government took power and refused to let him leave Kabul.

Najibullah, who had the stocky build of a wrestler, had been president when I first came to Afghanistan in 1986. He had been in the job one year by then. I had been drawn to Afghanistan by what I saw as the David-and-Goliath war being played out in this remote corner of the world. In 1986, the mujahedeen stood for the determined David and the Soviet army the militarily superior Goliath.

Afghanistan was being described as the Soviet Union's Vietnam. Ronald Reagan, keen to support a proxy war against America's Cold War enemy, had coined the phrase "freedom fighters" to describe the mujahedeen.

I was sure the battle was a pivotal one in the relationship between the United States and the Soviet Union, the world's two superpowers. And I wanted to see how it would play out.

No one expected that Afghanistan would be the last military confrontation of the Cold War or that the mujahedeen would so puncture the sense of Soviet invulnerability that soon one superpower would collapse utterly. Nor could anyone have imagined that Ronald Reagan's freedom fighters, whose Islamic fervor was being whipped up to a fever pitch to fight the godless Communists, would later become a deadly adversary of the United States and of the West. In 1986, most of the U.S. aid that came to Afghanistan went to the most radical of the mujahedeen factions because their fighters were the most daring, the most willing to face death in battle. They were also the mujahedeen groups that had within their ranks men like Osama bin Laden and his lieutenant, Aymen al-Zawahri.

I had arrived in Peshawar, Pakistan, in March 1986, having left behind fifteen years of working at newspapers in Canada. I sold everything I owned, which wasn't much, and set out to become the foreign correspondent I'd always wanted to be. The only way to get into Afghanistan then was to enlist the help of one of the seven main mujahedeen groups that were headquartered in Pakistan. One of them agreed to take me across the border. My first trip was in the company of one of the most radical of groups, Hezb-e-Islami, whose leader was the henna-bearded Maulvi Younis Khalis.

I struggled over several mountain passes, trudging behind donkey caravans loaded with weapons, spurred on by mujahedeen fighters. The occupying Red Army was in the middle of its biggest offensive. The soldiers had been given carte blanche by Soviet president Mikhail Gorbachev to exercise unrestricted brutality—to do whatever was necessary to destroy the mujahedeen resistance. There were more than 80,000 well-armed Soviet soldiers in Afghanistan.

The mountainsides were on fire. Napalm bombs pounded Afghanistan's eastern border with Pakistan, which was the staging arena for the resistance and the supply depot of weapons and ammunition financed by the United States and other Western countries.

We did most of our traveling by night, scaling wave after wave of mountain peaks that run like a seam along Afghanistan's border with Pakistan, cautiously making our way along narrow footpaths that snaked up the mountainsides.

Not far from the border, we came across a minefield. We had

no choice but to navigate through it. I put one foot in the exact same step as the mujahed in front of me. Progress was excruciatingly slow. I felt that I didn't dare to breathe, I was too afraid. Suddenly there was a loud explosion—it seemed as if it must be right next to me. I felt a nauseous surge of fear: The mujahed beside me had stepped on a mine. It killed him instantly.

The Afghan countryside was littered with explosives. Tens of thousands of small brightly colored land mines had been dropped from Russian aircraft, mostly along Afghanistan's southern and eastern borders with Pakistan. The cynical targets of these particular mines were children, hence the bright colors. The idea was not to kill but to maim, to force villagers, who were feeding and sheltering the mujahedeen, to flee Afghanistan in search of medical help for the injured children, thereby choking off their support to the mujahedeen.

Soviet aircraft could fly in low then. The mujahedeen's best weapon was the Sam-7 heat-seeking antiaircraft missile, which could be easily fooled and thrown off target by decoy flares dropped from the rear of a Russian aircraft. Occasionally, a mujahed would get off a lucky shot with a rocket-propelled grenade launcher and hit a helicopter gunship. But the upper hand was with the Soviet pilots.

I remember hiding beneath a clump of trees as a helicopter gunship hovered overhead. I knew their guns could cut us down. It was terrifying. Would they see us? Would they leave without firing? I could hear the whir of the blades. I tried to disappear inside the tree trunk.

The experience of the Soviets trying to subdue the Afghan mountains should have indicated to anyone who believed that it would be easy to capture bin Laden from his hideouts how wrong they were. I understand the difficulty of finding anyone in those forbidding mountains, whose hulking granite innards once saved my life. We were traveling on a bright sunny day, when suddenly the sound of a Russian bomber approached. I hid in one of the thousands of caves that burrow deep within the rock faces.

The Russian fighter jet flew low overhead, too low, I thought. I can still hear the drone of the engine, so close it seemed to be at my ear. My little hiding place was snug and I could just peek out. The pilot was flying so low I could see his face. He had fair hair. I was struck by the roundness of his face. He didn't see me, but when he bombed nearby, the earth shook with a ferocity that made me want to run out of my hiding place, to get somewhere, anywhere where I wouldn't feel like I was going to be buried alive. But I couldn't move. I just hugged the ground; shut my eyes so tight my head hurt. But the pilot never saw us, missed us even though we were right under his nose.

Toward the end of 1986, the United States gave the mujahedeen the weapon that would win them the war, the sophisticated Stinger antiaircraft missiles, which could lock in on an aircraft and not be diverted by decoy flares. The Stinger missiles forced the Soviet bombers and helicopter gunships to fly above an altitude of 20,000 feet. That meant the mujahedeen could move more freely, get more supplies in, ambush with greater success and cause the Soviet Union heavier losses, such as several multimillion-dollar fighter aircraft and gunships.

Like all the other weapons that came into Afghanistan for the mujahedeen, most of the Stingers were given to the most radical of Islamic guerrilla groups. Washington should have been nervous, though, because it wasn't long after the mujahedeen were given their first Stingers that some were sold to Iran. At the time, Washington denied it. But it happened: Some of the mujahedeen involved in the deal told me the story. Two Stingers were sold, handed over to the Iranians on the western border of Afghanistan. Several hundred thousand dollars exchanged hands.

But the mujahedeen made good use of the ones they didn't sell, which was most of them. It was the Stingers that finally forced the Soviets to the negotiating table.

The last Soviet soldier left Afghanistan in February 1989, abandoning Najibullah to his fate. He wasn't expected to survive, but he did. He held on for another three years, though his control grew progressively weaker. He withdrew to Afghanistan's cities, encircling each one with cordon upon cordon of security. Soon there was no coherent national government, just Najibullah and his troops in the cities and the mujahedeen in the countryside staking out territory.

Under Najibullah, Afghanistan's capital of Kabul, almost picturesque in the foothills of the Hindu Kush Mountains, thrived. There were concerts in an oval-shaped concert hall, in the Olympic-size stadium, and football games, and every year musicians from across the country congregated in the stadium, each in their own tiny corner playing their traditional music. During those festival nights, the stadium was ablaze with tiny fairy lights. Kabul University was packed with students, men and women, debating the Communist social order.

In the countryside, mujahedeen factions established areas of control based mostly on their ethnic background. They dealt in drugs and precious stones, and killed each other if their territory was threatened. Each of the seven big mujahedeen factions had hundreds of local commanders, who imposed their own rules in their own area, like little fiefdoms. Among the mujahedeen, anyone with four or more soldiers under his command was a commander. It was a system of medieval simplicity.

After the Soviet Union withdrew, the world's interest in Afghanistan flagged. When the Najibullah government didn't collapse, the international community did not have the wherewithal to deal with Afghanistan, plot its future, find sustainable leaders. World events quickly overshadowed Afghanistan. By the end of 1989, just months after the Soviet withdrawal, the Berlin Wall came crashing down, Reagan declared communism defeated, and the Soviet Union began to disintegrate. Afghanistan was yesterday's war. The wider world had done the most dangerous of things. It had stuffed this tiny country with massive amounts of weapons, including the precious Stingers, had turned over the countryside to the volatile discordant mix of mujahedeen factions, and then had walked away. For the United States, the war it was really interested in had been won; the proxy war was of little interest: The mujahedeen were the victors, the Communists were the losers. It didn't matter that the mujahedeen leaders had proved themselves to be murderous men who had signed and broken several accords. They vowed to put aside their territorial, ethnic, and religious divides, even traveling to Saudi Arabia to visit Mecca, Islam's holiest site, to seal their promise. But they never kept their promises. And no one cared.

Najibullah was forced to negotiate his own removal, and the mujahedeen were eventually given Kabul, despite their bitter rivalries and bloodletting. The task of negotiating this was handed over to the United Nations.

In April 1992, the United Nations fulfilled its mission and Najibullah agreed to step down, despite the fact that there was no coherent alternative government ready to replace him. No sustainable form of a mature government had been cobbled together. No one had even tried. The world had moved on without making even one attempt to find an alternative to the warfaring mujahedeen leaders. The United States wanted to give the spoils of its last Cold War battle to its mujahedeen allies and get out. The world had no interest in carefully assembling a unified government to rule Afghanistan, to rebuild and bring stability. That would have taken sustained involvement, and the forceful removal from the scene of some of the more vicious mujahedeen. Instead, the international community opted for a quick exit.

It was a ludicrous mistake to hand over Kabul to the mujahedeen. It set in motion the chaos that would eventually bring the Taliban to power. But the international community wasn't looking to Afghanistan's future. It wanted out.

And so Afghanistan was handed over to the fractious, feuding mix of tribal warlords, who had been elevated to the status of mujahedeen factional leaders to fight the Soviet Union. Their stature had been enhanced by the billions of dollars and weapons they had received from the United States and the rest of the world.

Their relentless internecine killing, their bloodletting over religious and tribal differences was ignored and they were given Kabul.

Afghanistan's first prime minister after Najibullah was Gulbuddin Hekmatyar, a towering Pashtun, whose Hezb-e-Islami faction had provided some of the strongest guerrilla fighters against the Soviet soldiers. Hekmatyar, whose deep-set eyes were dark and foreboding, was also the biggest opportunist among the leaders, and he would use religion, money, and guns all to achieve the same end—power. Hekmatyar was a radical Islamist, rarely hiding his loathing of the West and the United States even while he was the biggest recipient of U.S. dollars. As long as Hekmatyar's people killed Soviet soldiers, Washington decided to overlook his stream of anti-Western rhetoric.

Hekmatyar's biggest rival was Ahmed Shah Massood, Afghanistan's first post-Communist defense minister and an ethnic Tajik. The charismatic, French-speaking Massood had rarely left Afghanistan during the Soviet invasion. He was a pragmatic man who brokered truces with the Soviet forces and, in the early years of the Soviet invasion, cleansed ethnic Pashtuns from the valleys of the Hindu Kush Mountains of his homeland in order to solidify his power base in the north by ensuring that the Tajiks were unchallenged. He made hundreds of millions of dollars from the lucrative emerald and lapus lazuli mines. Massood held radical Islamic beliefs, was known to punish his men for not praying; his closest ally among the other mujahedeen leaders was Abdul Rasul Sayyaf, a radical Islamist who was tight with the Arab militants.

The only rival to Massood for full control of northern Afghanistan was Abdul Rashid Dostum, a stocky, mustachioed ethnic Uzbek, who remained a loyal Communist general under Najibullah until it seemed certain Najibullah would step down. Dostum then switched sides and joined the mujahedeen. His viciousness was legendary in Afghanistan.

These were the men the world installed in Kabul when Najibullah stepped down in April 1992. They were the mujahedeen "government."

They collided disastrously during their four years in power. It's a painful journey into those four years of Afghanistan's past, when the world handed a vibrant, intact Kabul over to the mujahedeen leaders, who destroyed it. But knowing the history of the early 1990s is essential because so many of the survivors of that era have recently been returned to power. Some have even been transformed into heroes. But among the Afghan mujahedeen leadership, there were no heroes.

To find a hero in Afghanistan you have to look to the 26 million ordinary Afghans, to men such as Amir Shah, an ethnic Hazara and one of Afghanistan's minority Shiite Muslims. Hazaras, with facial features like the rugged Mongolians of the Central Asian steppes, are on the bottom rung of the Afghan social ladder. Amir Shah's round face is open and kind and generous. He comes from Bamiyan, where the giant Buddha statues towered for centuries. Amir Shah has eight children, and a sprawling extended family.

Amir Shah's bravery takes my breath away, but it is his kindness and empathy for those who suffer around him that makes him a hero. He has seen his homeland through its many wars. He never considered abandoning it. When we first met, he was a taxi driver. A native Persian speaker with a high school education, Amir Shah laboriously taught himself English, writing down two or three words each day and at night poring over the words, memorizing them.

Amir Shah remembered the arrival of the mujahedeen in April 1992, and his initial hopes. "When the mujahedeen came to Kabul we hoped for our real Islam of peace, but soon everywhere there were preparations for war."

Before coming to Kabul, the mujahedeen leaders had signed an agreement that divided the ministries among the factions. Within months the agreement was torn up, and Massood had given the Interior Ministry to his friend Sayyaf, taking it away from the minority Shiite Muslims and driving them into Hekmatyar's camp.

Hekmatyar, still prime minister, refused to come into Kabul. Fearing the power of Massood and Sayyaf, he elected to corral weapons and men southeast of the capital at a place called Charasyab. There Hekmatyar waited, nurturing the ambition that he might soon control more than just the prime minister's role. From Charasyab, Prime Minister Hekmatyar threatened to destroy his own capital city, using Massood's new alliance with the ex-Communist Dostum as his excuse.

Kabul rapidly disintegrated into a battlefield, split into factional areas of control. Rival mujahedeen faced off against each other, sometimes no further apart than at opposite corners of the same street.

Together Amir Shah and I crisscrossed the front lines. He always kept a Quran on his car dashboard, carefully wrapped in a colorful silk scarf, always within easy reaching distance. Before crossing a dangerous area, Amir Shah would pick up the Quran, kiss it, and pray.

One front line between mujahedeen groups ran right outside the Kabul Zoo, which in another lifetime had been the best in Asia. The mujahedeen devastated it. They frightened or killed the animals, taking sadistic potshots at the elephants and bears in their compounds, and even at the caged animals. One black bear limped balefully after a chunk of shrapnel had been lodged in his burly paw. Rockets periodically slammed into the zoo buildings, into the cages, into the animals' watering holes.

The old man who ran the zoo throughout the mujahedeen fighting refused to leave his animals. The roof of the building in which he lived had been smashed in by a rocket, so a giant wall of cement slumped over the entranceway. To get in, you had to bend double and crawl between the fallen debris. But he stayed nonetheless, scavenging for food for himself and for his surviving animals. Anyone who came to his zoo, mostly visiting journalists, was asked to give money.

The most tenacious survivors were the lions. Marjan, an adult male, became a legend after surviving a grenade attack. It seems that a bored mujahed fighter decided one night to enter the lions' den. But Marjan didn't want company and saw the mujahed as a threat to the only female lion. Marjan circled the mujahed, trapped him and mauled him to death.

The next day, the mujahed's brother came looking for revenge. He skulked over to the lion's den, then waited for Marjan to be released from his cage into a large open space. In a single quick motion, the mujahed pulled the pin from his grenade and hurled it at Marjan. It struck the lion's face and exploded. Marjan was badly scarred and lost an eye and most of his teeth, but improbably, and rather like Afghanistan itself at that time, he survived.

Survival stories were treasured at that time because daily life for most ordinary men and women in Kabul was brutal and often unremittingly dangerous. Amir Shah had to watch as his home neighborhood was splintered by rocket attacks. "Dasht-e-Barchi was on fire. An old woman tried to flee. She begged me for help. But my car was packed with all my children and my wife. The children were sitting on top of each other. I had no room. I couldn't take her. I had to leave. I still see her face." His voice trailed off. Amir Shah is a kindhearted man who gives food each Friday to poor neighbors, prays at the shrine of saints, and rarely passes a beggar without giving a small donation. So, naturally, he returned to try to find the elderly woman. But he never did.

The rocketing between mujahedeen factions always seemed the heaviest in the morning, maybe because it startled you awake, sending you running to the basement for shelter. One particular morning, I decided to count the rockets. It wasn't easy—there were a lot. I tried to distinguish between the incoming rockets fired from Hekmatyar's positions in Charasyab and the nearby hills and the outgoing rockets from Massood's positions on other hills, including one just behind our house. In less than two minutes, I counted nearly 100 rockets. They were always accompanied by a spray of small-arms fire.

After a particularly blistering assault, we went to Amir Shah's Hazara neighborhood, where we found a man named Ghulam Jan collapsed over a brightly colored shawl. We couldn't see what was under it. Amir Shah talked to him, tried to comfort him. Sayyaf's men had stormed into the neighborhood and grabbed five women, including Ghulam Jan's wife. Ghulam Jan could barely talk. He threw open the shawl. Inside were long thick bunches of bloodied women's hair. I looked away. Ghulam Jan said Sayyaf's men raped the women, killed them, and then scalped them.

On another occasion, I stayed overnight in an apartment smack on the front line with a woman and her two small children. It was part of a sprawling complex of cement Stalinist-style apartment buildings that had been built by the former Soviet Union to house senior Communist government workers in a district called Macroyan. The woman's husband had fled several months earlier, fearing retribution from the mujahedeen government, because like many of the men who had apartments in Macroyan, he had worked for the Najibullah government.

He had been afraid to leave his family behind, but they didn't want to lose their apartment. On a hill directly behind their apartment building were Dostum's men, who fired rockets at another nearby hill, from where Massood's men retaliated, Dostum having switched allegiance once more, this time to become an ally of Hekmatyar.

Throughout the night, caught in the cross fire, we huddled together in the only room that did not have an outside wall. We thought it offered the best chance of safety, should the apartment take a direct hit. We braced ourselves against the wall. I tried to laugh with the children. The youngest, Maryam, was only seven. She had a shy smile, and her hair was long and matted. Her mother said she tried to keep it clean, but there was no running water and no electricity. Maryam helped her mother at a nearby bakery. Her brother was a stocky boy of ten. I wondered at how they could endure the rocketing night after night.

I watched them try to sleep. Maryam snuggled up to her

mother. She flinched and whimpered, but she managed to sleep. I don't know how; I couldn't. The reverberations from the exploding rockets continued relentlessly.

I was due to return to Pakistan the following morning. But before I left I went back to the apartment, bringing a bag of rice and flour with me. In the middle of the night, the woman had told me that she wanted to send her young son with me to Pakistan. She, too, was afraid, but she didn't want to lose her apartment. But by the time I returned, she had changed her mind. She couldn't bear to be separated from her son. He stayed.

Not much later, maybe three or four months, she and her two children were killed, their throats slit by men who belonged either to Massood's or Sayyaf's faction. They were killed for their apartment.

Such was the anarchy in Kabul during the mujahedeen's rule.

On yet another occasion, and during yet another firefight between rival mujahedeen factions, I returned to the same Macroyan subdivision. Just as I stepped from my vehicle, a volley of incoming rockets landed. I fled, trying to find a place to hide, unable to tell where they were coming from.

A little girl, maybe five years old, stepped out of one of the dirty gray cement buildings onto the stoop. She had come out to play. A rocket suddenly smashed into the ground in front of her. The powerful blast sent shrapnel searing through everything in its path, including the little girl. She died instantly.

The randomness of the violence was appalling. I visited a small boy no more than eight years old in the hospital in Kabul. He had been playing ball in his yard when a rocket smashed into the ground nearby, slicing off his hand at the wrist. Seconds before the rocket hit, he had reached out to catch the ball, and his hand was in midair when a razor-sharp piece of shrapnel sliced it off. When I saw the young boy, he was weeping silently, his tears rolling down his cheeks as his mother tried to comfort him.

Hospitals in Kabul were destroyed. Windows had no glass. Sheets of plastic whipped and buckled beneath the force of the icy winds that barreled down from the Hindu Kush Mountain range to the north. Sometimes operations had to be canceled because there was no anesthetic.

I once watched a man bleed to death on an operating table for lack of electricity and anesthetic. In the children's wards, tiny bodies, often wracked with coughing spasms, lay on dirty plastic mattresses in gray steel cribs set near oil-fired heaters to keep them warm. Black soot caked inside these children's delicate nostrils and their tiny lungs filled up with the fumes.

Land mines littered many neighborhoods in Kabul, placed there by the rival mujahedeen factions. In a single week in Kabul, as many as fifty people would die or be maimed by them. Mujahedeen groups booby-trapped entire neighborhoods. But the victims were usually the children, who scurried out whenever there was a lull in the fighting to scavenge and collect scrap to sell, or who had been sent by their parents to retrieve some essential items left behind during the heat of a battle. The mujahedeen were maliciously clever. They never booby-trapped the entrance to a home, where even the young knew to be cautious. Instead they would string the trip wire across a second-story staircase or at the entrance to a bedroom.

That thousands of innocent people died daily during the mujahedeen government was explained away one day by Sayyaf, who publicly said it would be better for the mujahedeen to raze Kabul and rebuild it in the image of their version of Islam. If that meant the death of many of the 1 million people living in Kabul, so be it, he said, explaining that they were Communists, or at least sympathizers, otherwise why would they have stayed in the city during Najibullah's rule?

I met Hekmatyar in Charasyab soon after Dostum had switched sides from Massood. I asked Hekmatyar how he could accept an ex-Communist general like Dostum after his reason for viciously rocketing Kabul earlier had been that Dostum was in the capital. Dostum in the meantime had gone to Saudi Arabia and performed the Muslim pilgrimage of Hajj and was known among Hekmatyar's men as Hajji Dostum.

"I change, you change, he changes. Everyone changes," said Hekmatyar without a hint of remorse. That was the extent of his explanation. But some things could never be changed: My mind filled with images of his victims and of the victims of all the mujahedeen leaders: the small children with limbs missing, the bodies mutilated by shrapnel; screaming mothers hugging their dead children; a cyclist ripped apart by shrapnel. There were so many.

I remembered visiting young girls in a Red Cross hospital and watching as they struggled with artificial limbs. They had been maimed by land mines and booby traps placed by the mujahedeen, and indirectly, I thought, by a Western world that had abandoned Afghanistan to the mujahedeen. Kabul, which had survived the Soviet occupation and survived Najibullah's siege mentality, was ultimately ruined by Western-armed mujahedeen. There seemed to be no unacceptable level of damage that would force the mujahedeen factions to stop fighting each other.

It wasn't until the summer of 1996, when the Taliban laid siege to Kabul, that the mujahedeen factions finally stopped their bloodletting and closed ranks against the Taliban.

The Afghan friend I have called Karim said that it was rumored at the time that bin Laden helped broker the reconciliation between Hekmatyar and Massood soon after his arrival in Afghanistan from Sudan in May 1996. Bin Laden had fought with Sayyaf during the Soviet invasion and so was close to Massood. At the same time, some of bin Laden's Arab warriors had fought alongside Hekmatyar. Bin Laden had links to both men. At the time of the reconciliation, bin Laden was in Jalalabad, protected by the mujahedeen government.

In June 1996, Hekmatyar came to Kabul for the first time since the mujahedeen takeover in 1992. He was sworn in as prime minister with due ceremony at the Intercontinental Hotel, which had been badly scarred by the relentless rocketing. It had no electricity or running water.

I watched the parade of unity from a wooden chair at the front of a cavernous hall that had been a ballroom during Najibullah's rule. All the mujahedeen leaders were on a stage. I marveled at their lack of conscience. There was Sayyaf, and beside him, Burhanuddin Rabbani, the titular president, who had agreed in 1992 to cede power after four months but held on for four years. As Rabbani's defense minister, Massood kept him in power. Hekmatyar stood by their side. They smiled, even kissed each other on the cheek.

I looked hard at the men on stage and at the couple of hundred men in the hall. Some of their faces I recognized: They were commanders whom I had seen on the front lines, some inside the city, and others on the hills that encircle Kabul. Between them all, they were responsible for the ruin of a once fine city, and for the deaths of more than 50,000 civilians. I thought at the time: "Now here is the biggest collection of mass murderers you'll ever get in one place." When I look around Kabul today, I see many of those same faces.

Hekmatyar was not allowed to enjoy the trappings of his newly official position for very long. The threat that had finally persuaded the rival mujahedeen factions to bury their differences was about to overwhelm them. By September, just four months after his swearing in, the Taliban were on Kabul's doorstep.

⚇

Shortly after 9 P.M. on September 26, 1996, Amir Shah picked me up at the United Nations guest house. The streets were deserted. We heard just token rocket and tank fire. Massood's soldiers were nowhere to be seen.

Amir Shah said he had watched them flee north out of the city under the cover of darkness. The mujahedeen, having ruined Kabul, had now abandoned it.

Najibullah, a bizarre survivor of a regime that had elsewhere vanished in the world, was still in the UN guest house. Sometime around 1 A.M. on September 27, he pleaded with the UN to help him because his security guards had fled. But no help came. The

Taliban dragged Najibullah and his brother from their UN compound, tortured and killed them, and then hung their bloated
bodies in the center of Kabul.

Around 4 A.M. on this same day, I awoke to the sound of the
Muslim call to prayer. It sounded extremely close, yet the nearest
mosque was several blocks away. I couldn't understand it until I
opened my window and looked down into the middle of the
street. There, a Taliban stood on the platform provided by a
tank; he was calling the faithful of the neighborhood to prayer.

CHAPTER TWO

Inside the Taliban

I first met Mullah Mohammed Khaksar in 1999, when the Taliban's hold on Afghanistan was unchallenged. They had consolidated their power through most of the country, and most of the world hated them.

By the time we met, Khaksar had lost his job as the Taliban's intelligence chief. As intelligence chief, he had been an important man, headquartered very close to Mullah Omar's office and home. The very powerful in Kandahar and within the Taliban movement would meet frequently at Khaksar's office. His star began to fade when he questioned Mullah Omar and openly expressed concern at the increasing involvement and ongoing presence of foreign fighters in Afghanistan.

Mullah Omar didn't take the criticism well. He transferred his former friend to Kabul and downgraded him to deputy interior minister. It was a comedown, but the new job wasn't without influence. As deputy interior minister, Khaksar oversaw the police, was responsible for security in the cities, and monitored the borders.

Khaksar was intimate with the Taliban. He saw up close the twists and turns the Taliban movement took, the manipulations it underwent at the hands of Arab militants, men like Osama bin

Laden, and at the hands of Afghans, trained in Pakistani religious schools called madrasses that were run by men who shared bin Laden's pan-Islamic visions, who held the same suspicions of the West, and whose strings were pulled by Pakistan's intelligence agency, which is deeply steeped in Islamic extremism.

Amir Shah precipitated my first meeting with Khaksar. The two had met several months earlier when Amir Shah had sought Khaksar's help to free an elderly uncle arrested by a cocky Taliban policeman. Like Amir Shah, his uncle, Hajji Jan, was an ethnic Hazara.

Because Amir Shah worked for a foreign organization, his family turned to him to find and free his uncle. They were in a panic, worried he would simply disappear, perhaps be killed, perhaps be forcibly drafted to fight with the Taliban.

Amir Shah asked Khaksar for help. It wasn't an easy thing to do. It took all of Amir Shah's courage just to enter the Interior Ministry in Kabul, which was encased behind a high wall. Unsmiling men swathed in black turbans and brandishing Kalashnikovs stood guard outside the rundown building. They didn't welcome any intrusion, least of all from a Hazara. It was a frightening place for him to go, but go he did.

As he walked through the grimy corridors, Amir Shah wondered about the wisdom of his decision. There was no electricity in the building and the only light came from occasional rays of sunshine piercing the dirt on the windows. He walked slowly, rarely making eye contact. Finally he found Khaksar's office. Chairs were lined up against the wall like sentries, and hugging one wall was Khaksar's heavy wooden desk, which seemed to fill the room.

Khaksar, wrapped in a large shawl to protect him from the cold, was smoking a cigarette. His holster was visible, a Kalashnikov rifle lay across his desk, and at his door were guards who looked like they could shoot you, throw your body into the trash, and casually go off for lunch.

The room was full of burly men with beards. They all seemed

to have something to ask Khaksar. Their faces were unsmiling. They didn't welcome a Hazara in their midst. Amir Shah, acutely aware of his vulnerability, wondered whether he would be able to speak.

Thankfully, Khaksar spoke first: "You have a problem?"

Amir Shah, a native Persian speaker, used his newly learned but still weak Pashtu. He was teaching himself the language because it was used by the Taliban, who came from the Pathan tribes in southern and eastern Afghanistan, and he could thus act as an interpreter for reporters.

Khaksar listened as Amir Shah told the story of his uncle's arrest. He didn't say much. When Amir Shah finished, Khaksar picked up the phone, made a few calls, found Hajji Jan and the truth behind the arrest. The Taliban policeman was a bully who was being mindlessly malicious. No crime had been committed, and so Khaksar ordered Amir Shah's uncle to be released.

But Khaksar's intervention didn't end there. He knew the mind of his young Pashtu policeman and was sure he would try to get his revenge from Hajji Jan when he thought Khaksar wasn't watching.

Khaksar made sure that didn't happen. He told the young policeman: "Arrest Amir Shah's uncle again and you will find yourself in jail."

Afghan jails are awful places regardless of the regime in power, but under the Taliban they were particularly unforgiving. The biggest and the most notorious is Pul-e-Charkhi prison, a crumbling institution that had been used by the Communist regime to torture anyone who disagreed with them. Many graves have been unearthed in the surrounding area.

The prospect of jail so frightened the young Taliban policeman that he went to Hajji Jan's house clutching a bouquet of bright red and white plastic flowers. Hajji Jan couldn't have been more surprised when he opened the steel gate to his compound to find a Taliban policeman with a bouquet, albeit a plastic one. Hajji Jan couldn't work out what was happening, half expecting that he must be about to be rearrested. Instead, the Taliban offered the flowers to the elderly Hazara along with an apology, before turning on his heels and leaving. It was a big moment for the elderly Hazara.

Hajji Jan's home is in one of the poorest neighborhoods of Kabul. In the best of times in Afghanistan, it would be rare for a Hazara to get a visitor from the ruling class, but to have a young Talib policeman make a visit with flowers and an apology—well, that is the stuff that legends are made of.

Amir Shah remains grateful to Mullah Khaksar: "I will never forget him for that. In those days he was a very big man. He didn't even have to talk to me, but he did and he made it right for my family. He saved my uncle." He laughs a little. "He also made me a hero with my family."

৪৯৪

Mullah Mohammed Khaksar knows the Taliban's origins because he was one of the founders of the movement. He saw the organization blossom and watched it strengthen in response to the violent anarchy of the mujahedeen commanders-cum-warlords.

When the Taliban themselves were driven out of Kabul in 2001, Khaksar stayed behind. Leaving with the Taliban wasn't the answer. Khaksar had helped create the Taliban in 1994 for the same reason that he refused to leave Kabul no matter what the risk to himself in 2001: "I just want peace. I have wanted peace since the Taliban began."

When the Taliban fled, Khaksar didn't try to change his appearance. Although everyone else in Kabul seemed to be rushing to get rid of their beard and *shalwar kameez*—the traditional outfit of baggy pants and long tunic worn by men—to exchange them for a Western-style suit and tie, Khaksar remained as he was. His beard stayed long and shaggy, streaked with gray, and he wore his turban.

Khaksar remained what he was: A devout cleric who had fought against invading Russian soldiers, then returned to his home in Kandahar when they withdrew and their Communist protégés in Kabul were defeated, only to discover that the country had not been delivered from tyranny or warfare. So he returned to fight against the feuding mujahedeen groups that had turned his country into an anarchic and criminal wasteland.

Those were brutal years for Afghanistan. The Taliban arrived in response to that brutality, Khaksar said, while never denying that the Taliban had in their time become a repressive regime, too. But that was not their original intention.

"People should look at the good and the bad of the Taliban," Khaksar once said to me. "The good was the peace and the security that the Taliban brought. But the bad was the foreigners—the Arabs and Pakistani fighters—and the strict pressures that the Taliban imposed."

He once counted Mullah Omar among his friends. Today Mullah Omar wants him dead. Khaksar is strangely sanguine about the threat. But then, in the many conversations I have had with him about the Taliban, he has often mocked the Western preoccupation with Mullah Omar and the media's desire to portray him as a stereotypical arch-villain, an evil tyrant, a maniacal one-eyed radical.

Khaksar saw him differently. He knew Mullah Omar's origins. He knew the man he was as well as the man he became, from the time when he was a guerrilla fighter against invading Soviet troops. He knew Omar before he became the Taliban leader personified in the eyes of the Western world.

Mullah Omar's beginnings were humble, his kingdom a small mud mosque in a place called Sanghisar in the Panjwali District of southern Afghanistan. He was a simple man, not well educated, as he had been schooled only at a village madrassa, receiving introductory study of the Quran and little else. Nor had he become a deep, intellectual thinker. Khaksar, an avid reader, was the one who loved to talk about Islam and its teachings. Mullah

Omar wasn't a big talker. He spoke in measured sentences, his speech often painfully slow. His interpretation of the Quran was literal, basic. As Khaksar said: "You could never doubt Mullah Omar's love of the Quran, of Islam. He didn't know deep meanings, but he loves Islam, he loves the Quran."

Mullah Omar wore his deep black beard long and scraggy. His head was always swathed in the traditional turban, as it is in the only picture of him that I have ever seen—a fuzzy old photograph taken when he was a mujahedeen warrior fighting the invading Soviet army.

During the Taliban's rule, Mullah Omar banned photography, but when he was a mujahedeen, Khaksar said, Mullah Omar would often pose for the camera. Khaksar once had many pictures of the one-eyed Taliban leader, but fleeing Taliban soldiers destroyed them.

Legends have grown up around Mullah Omar, one being that the one-eyed mullah removed his own eye after being hurt in a particularly blistering ambush against a Soviet military convoy. According to the legend, a convoy of Soviet and Afghan soldiers was rumbling south to Kandahar. Mullah Omar was among the mujahedeen who ambushed the convoy with hand grenades, rocket launchers, and small-arms fire. The mujahedeen were hopelessly overpowered by the elite Russian commandos, who were protected by armored vehicles and tanks. Tank fire smashed into the mujahedeen lines. Bullets screamed overhead. The sharp whine of a rocket was one of the last sounds Mullah Omar heard before a piece of shrapnel pierced his eye. The pain was excruciating. Using the bayonet knife attached to the barrel of his Kalashnikov rifle, Omar removed the piece of shrapnel and with it, his useless eye—or so the story goes.

The truth is that Omar did indeed lose his eye in battle, but the gory self-surgery with a bayonet is an invention. He was stitched up at a clinic in Kandahar, according to Taliban who knew him.

The Taliban's beginnings, like those of its leader, Mullah

Omar, were humble and not expansionist in nature. The Taliban when it began was not a pan-Islamic movement with terrorist intentions. That came later.

Sixty men founded the Taliban, according to Khaksar. In the final years of the Taliban, more than half of the founding fathers, had either died or returned to their mosques, disillusioned with the Taliban they had helped to create.

At first the Taliban was a nationalist movement created to tackle anarchy and lawlessness. Khaksar has grown deeply tired of the repeated litany of errors about the origins of the Taliban, about Mullah Omar and his relationship with Osama bin Laden.

Let me tell you, the foreign countries got it all wrong about the beginning of the Taliban. It wasn't created by Pakistan, or by the Arabs, or by the Americans. From the beginning, the world was wrong about the Taliban.

For example, some people said that the Americans brought the Taliban; and some people said Pakistani intelligence brought the Taliban; and some said the Arabs brought them. But all of these things were wrong. The Taliban came because there was so much corruption, and people were killing each other, and mujahedeen commanders had become like thousands of little kings. Then, everyone was a commander.

The Taliban was subsequently exploited by many foreign forces, but in 1994 it was just a group of angry men, looking for an end to the lawlessness.

Mullah Omar didn't often leave his small crumbling village mosque, made of mud and straw, but when he did he would encounter mujahedeen commanders demanding money. They would stick a gun in his face, order him to pay a road tax or be killed.

Mullah Omar's ambitions were small. They didn't stretch far beyond a local stretch of the highway. Mullah Omar wanted to rid a forty-kilometer stretch of road from his village of Sanghisar to Kandahar of the marauding band of thieves that held it hostage. Mujahedeen commanders had set up checkpoints every ten kilometers, collecting what they called "road taxes." What the mujahedeen commanders didn't steal, common criminals did. The Taliban was born out of anger and frustration with the thieving mujahedeen commanders, who had become old-fashioned highway robbers.

In 1994, robberies were routine occurrences on Afghanistan's highways. Buses often carried extra supplies just to bribe the mujahedeen commanders they knew would stop them. On three different occasions, the Associated Press had its satellite telephones stolen by commanders loyal to Gulbuddin Hekmatyar, always on the road between Jalalabad and Kabul in eastern Afghanistan.

Mullah Omar hadn't harbored dreams of starting a government. Once the Soviets left Afghanistan in 1989 and the Communist government collapsed in 1992, Mullah Omar returned to his mosque and to teaching the Quran to village boys, who would sit on the mud floor while their one-eyed teacher lectured them on the tenets of Islam. Mullah Omar had returned to a simple life.

His decision to try to get rid of the thieving commanders came after he made a particularly horrific trip to Kandahar from his village of Sanghisar. The roads hadn't been repaired and his rickety car bumped and banged along the road, barely picking up speed before it was forced to stop at yet another checkpoint.

The checkpoints were rarely elaborate. A few men with guns would step out into the middle of the road, which was sometimes blocked by a spindly piece of wood.

On this particular trip, Mullah Omar was stopped five times by five different commanders. He knew them all. He had fought with them during the 1980s. Now they were no more than thieves demanding their "road tax."

He paid bribe after bribe, and the more he paid, the more enraged he became. When he finally reached Kandahar, he had decided to take on the men he had once called his comrades-in-arms.

If the road leading to Kandahar had been a nightmare, the city itself was even worse. In a single day, for instance, gun battles between rival mujahedeen commanders had left forty-two people dead. No one was safe, not even the United Nations, which once had to negotiate for the return of an entire food convoy.

Kandahar in 1994 was ruled by a *shura,* a collection of old men whose tribal lineage had put them in a position of power. The *shura* was akin to a town council. But they were powerless. They would hold regular meetings, bemoan the sorry state of affairs, and return to their homes. They had no army with which to impose order. Their rulings were rarely implemented.

One of the biggest crooks and the most powerful man in Kandahar then was Gul Aga Sherzai, who was restored to power in 2001 by the United States, and who today, as governor of Kandahar Province, sits beside Hamid Karzai. For a brief time Karzai tried to relocate him to Kabul as a government minister, but it didn't last. Sherzai wanted his lucrative Kandahar back, and he got it by making it impossible for the Karzai-appointed man to run the province.

Back in 1994, Sherzai was one of the biggest dealers in drugs and contraband. His greedy men included those administering the roadblocks, from which Sherzai received a share of the take.

Mullah Omar looked first to other mullahs for support. He found sixty willing men, all of them mullahs and all from the Pashtun tribes of southern Afghanistan.

Khaksar said Mullah Omar bore no particular grudge against the *shura* elders, but they were ineffectual in combating the wholescale corruption: "We weren't against the Kandahar *shura,* but they were old and weak and had no control over the criminals."

Mullah Omar first called a tribal *jirga*—a council of important men—composed of sixty of his fellow mullahs. Their first order of business was to empower themselves by getting hold of money and weapons. They all agreed they wanted to get rid of the checkpoints. They didn't have any grand scheme, and there wasn't really a plan beyond that objective. It was all very parochial.

Some of the mullahs were prominent men in Kandahar. They had some money, and everyone had a Kalashnikov rifle at home—some even had rocket launchers from their days as anti-Soviet warriors.

Mullah Omar wasn't looking to be the leader. He was ready to hand that job over to anyone who wanted it. But from mullah to mullah they went, and they decided that the humblest among them was Omar and he should be allowed to lead.

Some made donations right then and there. Khaksar gave a direct donation to Mullah Omar—50,000 Afghanis (about $10, at a time when a doctor in Afghanistan was making $16 a month) to help launch the movement, to fight the corrupt warlords.

> The truth was that we didn't know where the Taliban would go. We didn't begin it with the idea of taking over the country.
>
> In my country then, robberies and insecurity were a fact of everyday life. There was no peace; there was only fear and corruption. You couldn't go down the road without someone demanding money and putting a gun in your face if you didn't give it to him.
>
> For truck drivers it was a full day's drive just to go 100 kilometers because of all the checkpoints. They looted everything, and if they didn't steal from you, they demanded a bribe from you. In the beginning the Taliban began to get rid of these things and these people.

At the first *jirga*, the mullahs collected money. Then they decided to take on a single checkpoint. There were plenty to choose from, but Mullah Omar wanted to tackle a particular one not far from his village, the one run by Commander Saleh. He had been exceptionally mean and vicious.

The plan was simple: attack and shut it down or die trying. They were ready for a fight. The mullahs-turned-vigilantes launched a frontal assault. Some of them had taken up positions in nearby hills to offer covering fire. They were ready to do battle, but there wasn't one: "Commander Saleh and his men just ran. Everyone was surprised that they didn't stay and fight. We thought it was going to be a big fight. When we won so easily we decided to go to the next checkpoint."

Nobody debated the decision—there was no time and no need. The mullahs dismantled Saleh's checkpoint, took the rocket launchers and Kalashnikov rifles the fleeing men had left behind, and set out for the next checkpoint, barely ten kilometers away.

It became a game of dominoes, one checkpoint after the other collapsed, the gunmen fleeing as the mullahs pressed on. It didn't take more than a few days before all the checkpoints strung along the road from Mullah Omar's Sanghisar village to Kandahar were gone—and the Taliban movement was born.

Initially, the movement had no name. No one had thought it needed one. But as their progress gathered momentum, many new recruits joined the mullahs and most came from the local religious schools where Omar and his fellow mullahs taught. So Omar took the Arabic name Talib, meaning student, and adopted it for his movement. The name had been used briefly during the Soviet invasion, when a small force had called itself Taliban, but they had disbanded when the Soviet Union pulled out. It took Mullah Omar to reinvent it.

Khaksar said not only did the world get it wrong about the origins of the Taliban, but it also got it wrong about Mullah Omar and his links to Osama bin Laden. And the U.S. intelligence apparatus got it wrong.

Since September 2001, Mullah Omar has been widely portrayed as an old friend of Osama bin Laden's. Richard C. Clarke, the CIA counterintelligence chief, said that Mullah Omar and bin Laden were old friends and that Mullah Omar was anxious for bin Laden to return to Afghanistan from Sudan. Khaksar denies this, saying the two had never met until after the Taliban took control of Kabul in September 1996.

Clarke said Bin Laden was encouraged by Mullah Omar to come to Afghanistan from Sudan to build training camps and bring his money. That's plain wrong. The terrorist training camps flourished under the mujahedeen government, the opponents of the Taliban. Osama bin Laden came to Afghanistan from Sudan with the help of the mujahedeen government.

The Taliban had become, by 2001, a loathsome repressive regime. But that does not justify or explain why the CIA revised history in order to connect bin Laden and Mullah Omar in those early days of the Taliban movement. The CIA should have known that Osama bin Laden's friends were the men of the Northern Alliance, men like Abdul Rasul Sayyaf, the very men it would later choose to help hunt bin Laden.

"Mullah Omar didn't know Osama during the jihad. During the holy war [against the Soviet Union] Osama never came to Kandahar. There were some Arabs who were in Kandahar during the jihad, but it was less than in other places. Maybe thirty Arabs would be there at any one time. They fought in different bunkers with different groups. They would come and go. Sometimes they would stay for a little while and other times they would just come for an operation and then go," Khaksar told me.

I believed him because his description exactly matched my own experience in Kandahar in 1986. Not once did I see an Arab fighter in several trips to Kandahar province. Furthermore, when the mujahedeen in Kandahar spoke of Arab fighters they did it with derision, always ready to take their money but never counting them as friends.

The mujahedeen helped me sneak into Kandahar in 1986 when the Soviets were still directing their war in Afghanistan. I was hidden beneath a burqa, that voluminous covering that provided only a mesh from which to peer out. Kandahar Province looked as though it had been hit by a nuclear bomb. Acre upon acre of orchards had been destroyed. The villages, such as Argandaub, where Mullah Omar had fought, had been flattened by the relentless bombing.

It's a bizarre twist that the Taliban movement, with its horrific repressiveness and abhorrence of music and mysticism, should have come out of Kandahar, where ritual worship at shrines is widespread. That region is home to the Pirs, clerics who trace their lineage to Islam's prophet and have mystical qualities that are revered, their feet and hands kissed.

The severe interpretation of Islam that the Taliban eventually embraced with such vigor came from the outsiders who would take it over, the Afghans trained at Pakistani madrassas, and later by the austere philosophy of Wahabi Islam practiced by Saudi Arabia and the Arab militants who would later wield such control.

Kandahar was not a city of severe Islam in 1986. Kandaharis were not anti-Western ideologues, but in fact just the opposite. The mujahedeen, who arranged my clandestine visit to Kandahar city, were Pashtun tribesmen, kinsmen of Mullah Omar. They drove throughout the region on motorcycles.

In their homes in bomb-shattered villages were old dust-clogged tape recorders that blared Pashtu songs. The most popular singer was a Pashtu chanteuse named Nagma, who sang of love lost, new love.

Music screamed from a tape recorder in the bus that took me and the young wife and mother of a mujahed to Kandahar on that secret visit. I couldn't even speak for fear of giving myself away—I didn't know any Pashtu.

The first thing we did when we disembarked fifteen painful kilometers later was to pray at one of Kandahar's most famous shrines, the Shrine of the Cloak of the Prophet.

The arid flat plain on which Kandahar was built is searingly hot in the summer and like a desert in the winter—hot during the day and freezing cold at night. Kandaharis believe the searing heat is punishment from a 300-year-old saint named Babar Farid, who had heard that the people of Kandahar had become selfish and unkind to strangers. He tested them and found them uncharitable. He punished them by calling down the sun that fried the earth and the people living there. Kandaharis learned their lesson, and the rules of hospitality are faithfully adhered to even though each year in the summer the sun still burns fiercely.

Kandahar's architecture is utilitarian, except for its shrines, which are magnificent. The Shrine of the Cloak of the Prophet is a stunning building of green marble and sparkling tile work.

From there, I was hurried to the home of a mujahedeen collaborator. The walls were crowded with pictures of family members, all men. The Taliban would later ban photographs, which was another incongruity. Afghans love to have their picture taken, and nowhere is that more true than in Kandahar.

While we sat on the floor of my host's home for about half an hour waiting for a meal to be prepared, talking about the Soviet invaders and their Communist Afghan allies, we were surprised by a knock on the door. The men around me spoke fast, and suddenly my women companions grabbed their burqa and mine. We had been discovered. People had begun to hear rumors of a foreigner in Kandahar.

We moved quickly. We ran from the house and jumped into a waiting rickshaw that weaved us through the narrow streets. It stopped suddenly. One of the women grabbed me, and in a heartbeat we climbed onto the back of a horse-drawn cart that clomped its way through the city. And that way, we escaped undetected.

When the Taliban's repressive restrictions began to emerge, I wondered how they could come from Kandahar. It contrasted so dramatically to my memories of music-loving Kandaharis, who would fly kites even in the middle of their war-ravaged villages, who went to shrines to pray for everything from a baby boy to a cure for insomnia.

The repressiveness did not belong to the Kandahar I remembered but rather to the Wahabi sect of Islam, about which Kandaharis had always spoken so disparagingly.

According to Khaksar, not only was Osama bin Laden not in Kandahar during the Soviet occupation of Afghanistan, when finally he met Mullah Omar in Kabul in 1996, but it was not at Omar's instigation. Instead, it was Osama Bin Laden who made a careful, deferential approach:

> During the holy war Osama was in Kunar, Khost, Laghman, and Jalalabad. The first time Mullah Omar met Osama was after the Taliban captured Kabul. Then it was Osama who wanted to come to meet Omar and come to Kandahar. Mullah Omar didn't call Osama to Kandahar.
>
> The Arabs didn't know what Mullah Omar would do. There were some tensions in the beginning between the Taliban and the Arabs, because when the Taliban captured Maidan Shahr west of Kabul, some of the Arabs were fighting with Hekmatyar. Osama sent a message when the Taliban captured Kabul requesting to see Mullah Omar.

Osama actually sweetened his message to Omar with a poem. It went something like this:

> There is no lion in the world, only Maulvi Khalis,[1] because
>   you gave me shelter,
> There is no better place in the world than Kandahar because,
>   Mullah Omar, you have announced Sharia[2] and you are
>   the hero of Islam.

---

1. Maulvi Younis Khalis led a breakaway faction of Hezb-e-Islami and was a key mujahedeen leader who welcomed bin Laden to Afghanistan from Sudan. He became mujahedeen education minister, and his men were foolishly used by the U.S. to track bin Laden after 9/11.

2. Sharia is Islamic law.

CHAPTER THREE

The Beginning of the End

In early 1995, Mullah Omar sat in a simple house in Kandahar in a stark room whose brown walls were naked but for a single verse from the Quran. Written in extravagant calligraphy, it urged the faithful to stay on the straight and narrow path and resist temptation. His six-foot frame rested against a big oval pillow covered in red velvet.

He wasn't alone. On the carpeted floor, leaning their bulky frames against the same plush velvet pillows were fifteen bearded men. They wore the traditional *shalwar kameez* and spoke in Mullah Omar's native Pashtu. But they weren't from Afghanistan.

They were all Pakistanis, powerful clerics who operated some of the biggest madrassas in Pakistan. They had come to position themselves as the godfathers of the young Taliban movement.

They had already contributed foot soldiers to the Taliban, students who were pressed into service with promises of a heavenly paradise, should they die fighting with the Taliban. They piled them into trucks and sent them across the border to shore up the Taliban's ranks against the mujahedeen. Some of the schools had even declared a jihad break, canceling classes to let the students take up arms in Afghanistan.

Mullah Omar was willing to embrace anyone who swore allegiance to the Quran. By the hundreds, Afghan refugee boys who had been studying in Pakistan signed up. Mullah Omar didn't care whether the new recruits were Afghan and he also welcomed the hundreds of Pakistani students, who were filled with the spirit of jihad. They went into battle with a Kalashnikov in one hand and a Quran in the other.

Resistance was sporadic and rarely fierce, and by early 1995, the Taliban were in control of several provinces in the south and east of Afghanistan. The roads were swept clean of the checkpoints and commanders-cum-warlords, who either joined the Taliban or fled, some to Pakistan and some to other provinces. The Taliban were on the move.

The Pakistani clerics who had gathered that day in Mullah Omar's house were known to each other. They were men with a vision that didn't recognize borders but sought to unite all Muslim countries under one banner of radical Islam.

But Mullah Omar's ambitions were much simpler. For Mullah Omar, his Taliban were the means by which he could bring security to his deeply anarchic country, and disarm and disband the unruly and lawless mujahedeen.

The Pakistani mullahs had much experience of insurgencies. Their schools were the breeding ground for jihadis, young religious zealots ready to do battle for their faith and die in its name. The Pakistani mullahs who gathered at Mullah Omar's carried the banner of jihad, taught its value at their schools, its requirement under Islam.

And behind them, propping them up with money and weapons were Pakistan's military and its secret service, which had been using the students and their Islamic fervor to wage Pakistan's proxy wars ever since the young jihadis had emerged as a force during the resistance to the Soviet occupation of Afghanistan. In 1992, when Afghanistan was handed over to the mujahedeen government, Pakistan's military pressed the student jihadis into service to fight its enemy India in the disputed Kashmir region. Also, the Pakistani mullahs had contributed students to Bosnia to fight against the Serbs, to Chechnya to fight against Russia, and some had even mixed with the Uighurs in the northwestern corner of China, stirring up their Islamic passions. Almost anywhere there was an Islamic insurgency, the mullahs rushed to contribute foot soldiers.

One of the most powerful among them was Nizamuddin Shamzai, a gray-bearded mullah who ran one of Pakistan's biggest madrassas, buried deep within the maze of streets of Karachi, a massive city of 15 million people on the shores of the Arabian Sea. Shamzai's students revered him almost as a saint.

As the Taliban intelligence chief, Mohammed Khaksar was present at the 1995 meeting. He already knew some of the Pakistani mullahs. As was his habit, Mullah Omar wasn't saying much, just listening.

Khaksar heard each mullah attempt to flatter Mullah Omar by associating the humble Taliban leader with the great spiritual icons of Islam. Mullah Omar believed that messages were delivered to the holiest in dreams, and those present knew he had once said he had a dream in which the prophet applauded him for sorting out Afghanistan's warlords. Thus, the mullahs proffered their best inventions, as Khaksar told it:

> The first mullah said to Mullah Omar: "I dreamt that the Prophet Mohammed was with you"; and then another said, "No, I dreamt that Hazrat Ali was with you"; and another said, "No, but the other night I dreamt that Hazrat Uzman was with you"; and yet another said, but "in my dream I saw Hazrat Omar with you." Finally after the seventh mullah told Mullah Omar his dream, I shouted: "Stop, enough."
>
> I couldn't listen to any more. I asked Mullah Omar to let me talk to these people. I said to them: "We have found a person who is good and who is bringing security and who is fighting against corruption. This is good. Don't talk about these false dreams. All this talk of dreams will perhaps do harm to this man. Instead, if you want, then say that this

work is good, or this work is bad, or this will make things better for Afghanistan, but don't feed him these wrong things about visions and dreams."

It wasn't the first time Pakistani clerics had met Mullah Omar. But previously they had come in small groups of two, sometimes three. They would praise him for his interpretation of Islam, for his imposition of a strict and unforgiving interpretation of Islamic Sharia law. But the large gathering in Kandahar was part of a grander scheme by the Pakistani military and its intelligence service, the ISI, to wield control over the Taliban by using both the mullahs and the jihadis. The Taliban, as Khaksar realized, were naive:

Then we didn't mind who joined with us. Everyone was welcome and from Pakistan hundreds of Talibs came. But the Pakistani military men and their intelligence were not running the Taliban. They were not in control then. Pakistan was sending just fighters, and Mullah Omar said: "OK. Anyone who wants to fight against corruption is welcome." There were Afghan Talib and Pakistani Talib. Lots of fighters came from Pakistan. There were trucks full of Talib. Under the name of Muslims, everything was accepted by the Taliban.

The Taliban had first impressed the Pakistani Secret Service (ISI) in October 1994, when they recovered a trade convoy that Pakistan was trying to move through Afghanistan to Central Asia. Mujahedeen commanders had hijacked it, and demanded a ransom.

Nasrullah Babaar, Pakistan's interior minister and an ethnic Pashtun, had staked his reputation on getting the convoy through Afghanistan. The naysayers in Pakistan had scoffed at the idea of using lawless Afghanistan as a trade route to Central Asia. Babaar thought he could confront the Pashtun mujahedeen commanders, but his confidence was misplaced.

The Taliban offered to recover the convoy from the wayward commanders. In charge of the convoy's security was a Pakistani colonel named Imam, a shadowy ISI man who espoused radical Islam and loathed the West and the United States. Imam saw the potential in the Taliban, and under his guiding hand the Pakistani military and its secret service set out to take it over.

The Taliban had a lot to offer Pakistan. They could provide strong Pashtun allies in Afghanistan, something Pakistan desperately needed because its only other significant Pashtun ally was Gulbuddin Hekmatyar, the mujahedeen prime minister who hadn't yet set foot in Kabul, choosing to stay outside the city and pound it with rockets in an attempt to dislodge his rival and the current defense minister, Ahmed Shah Massood.

Pakistan had been supplying Hekmatyar with money and weapons. It wanted Hekmatyar and ethnic Pashtuns to be the dominant power in the mujahedeen government, but they seemed to have little chance of dislodging Massood and the president, Burhanuddin Rabbani, both of whom were Tajiks. Pakistan hoped the Taliban could change that.

The Taliban could also provide training and inspiration for the jihadis that Pakistan was using with such ferocity in Indian-ruled Kashmir, a small former princedom that both India and Pakistan claimed as their own.

Pakistan wanted Mullah Omar to remain at the head of the Taliban. His single-minded devotion to the Quran and the simplicity of his obsession with a strict and literal interpretation offered a powerful living symbol around which they could fire up the jihadi spirit.

Never before, even among the strictest and most orthodox Wahabis, had there been a movement that ordered its followers to live as Islam's prophet had lived in the seventh century—the same clothes, the same style of beard, even the same style of turban. Mullah Omar looked as Islam's prophet must have looked. He lived as Islam's prophet had. He was held out as the purest of Islamic leaders.

It wasn't difficult to co-opt the Taliban. Pakistan insinuated its control slowly and insidiously. It used Pakistani mullahs like those attending the meeting in Kandahar to mold and manipulate Mullah Omar. Additionally, the ISI recruited Afghans trained at Pakistani madrassas to infiltrate Mullah Omar's inner circle. One of Pakistan's handpicked men was Tayyab Aga, barely thirty-five years old and a perfect English speaker. He would eventually become Mullah Omar's spokesman, rarely leaving his side. He won Mullah Omar's confidence through sheer persistence.

Every day, he and his friends would sit outside Mullah Omar's office in Kandahar and send in messages, pleading to see the one-eyed leader. Mullah Omar didn't always answer their messages. Sometimes they waited weeks before being called in to see him. But they were patient men.

Each time, they would fill his head with flattery, praising him for his commitment to Islam, to the purity of the Sharia law that he had imposed. The seduction went on for months.

A measure of their progress was that eventually some of the founding members of the Taliban, men like Khaksar, had trouble seeing Omar. Khaksar said: "It changed slowly. I used to walk into his office unannounced, drink tea and talk. But then it changed. I couldn't easily see him. He was always too busy and when we did get in they were always there, these mullahs from Pakistan or these new Afghan mullahs talking nonsense."

The real triumph for Pakistan and for its Afghan surrogates came in the first months of 1996 on the day that Mullah Omar removed the Cloak of Islam's Prophet from its sacred resting place, unseen since 1935, and in front of more than 1,500 mullahs who had traveled to Kandahar, declared himself Amir-ul Momineen, or King of the Faithful.

This act of hubris turned even the Muslim countries against the Taliban, reducing their circle of international friends and making them more dependent on Pakistan. It also inspired the Islamic zealots, those jihadis Pakistan had been nurturing so carefully.

At this time the Taliban were in control of several provinces and were still feeling the glow of the capture of western Herat, which was the first non-Pashtun province to have fallen under their control. The capture of Herat sent an unmistakable message: It removed any notion that the Taliban would restrict their cleanup operations to Pashtun regions of Afghanistan, making it clear that the Taliban wanted control of the entire country.

The Kandahar assembly of clerics was intended to solemnize the Taliban movement. It was to show that the Taliban had the support of the religious elite from across Afghanistan, not just the south of the country.

Mullah Omar seemed almost a spectator at the meeting. It was chaos. Everyone wanted a say. They talked for hours.

Mullah Khudaidad had come to Kandahar from eastern Khost. Khudaidad scratched his unruly beard as he recollected the meeting. He had traveled with several friends:

> We were talking with each other and we all wondered what Mullah Omar wanted from us. We hadn't been told much except to come to Kandahar. Until then I hadn't seen Mullah Omar, but I knew of him from a Kandahari mullah who had been with us in our madrassa. We knew that he was a mujahed and that he lost his eye in the jihad. When we arrived, he still wasn't there. Then four people came in a white-colored car, one was Mullah Omar, and we were told later one was Tayyab Aga, Mullah Omar's personal assistant, and the other two were bodyguards.

Mullah Dadullah, a former mujahedeen commander who had joined the Taliban, limped up to the podium, dragging his wooden leg behind him. Dadullah was fierce looking, with a long unkempt beard and thickly wrapped turban that sat just above his bushy eyebrows. Dadullah's reputation as a warrior against the Soviet soldiers was legendary, and it was well known that his relations with the Pakistani intelligence were solid. They had given generously to Dadullah during the anti-Soviet jihad.

Until that day there had been no public talk of Amir-ul Momineen other than among the small circle that orchestrated his ascension. But the direction changed. Khaksar, who had been in charge of security of the meeting, said some of the mullahs began to talk about Mullah Omar as Amir-ul Momineen, King of the Faithful, worldwide.

I said to Mullah Omar that day: "Be careful."

After hours of talking, they declared Mullah Omar [to be] Amir-ul Momineen. It was an unfair thing to do to Mullah Omar. It was Pakistan that wanted this. They were not trying to help him and to help Afghanistan. They wanted to turn the world against us. They wanted to keep Mullah Omar alone and to make the rest of the world, even the Muslim world, against him. It was a betrayal of Mullah Omar. When it was announced that he was Amir-ul Momineen, it meant that he was Amir of Muslims all over the world, and of course the Muslim world complained. How could one man say he is Amir of all Muslims? What gave him the right?

When Mullah Omar said he was Amir-ul Momineen, it was as if we had put a big wall between us and other Muslims. I knew that among these ulema, religious leaders, were mullahs who were working for Pakistan, who were intentionally trying to create problems for Mullah Omar, with other Islamic countries and with the rest of the world. Mullah Omar didn't understand that they wanted the world against him. They wanted Afghanistan to be alone in the world because then they would be in control. Mullah Omar just couldn't see this.

Mullah Khudaidad said there were some at the gathering who didn't agree with Mullah Omar declaring himself Amir-ul Momineen. They questioned such a simple mullah taking on such a grand title. But Khudaidad said everyone at the gathering was fed up with the mujahedeen, wanted them gone, and knew that Mullah Omar had Pakistan's support. Money and weapons were coming across the border from Pakistan. Khudaidad knew it because a lot was moving through his home city of Khost. It was also coming through at other border crossings, at Torkham and Kunar. "People there were talking about Pakistan's help and Nasrullah Babaar helping the Taliban and people said they were getting lots of money from Saudi Arabia and the United Arab Emirates. That made Mullah Omar very strong," Khudaidad said.

Mullah Omar eventually spoke to the gathering. His words came slowly, almost painfully slowly. Each one seemed to come a minute apart from the next.

Mullah Khudaidad recalled Omar's speech. He told the gathering: "I started the Islamic movement in Afghanistan because the mujahedeen were using the name of Islam and they were playing with this name."

To answer the mujahedeen government's accusation that Pakistan was masterminding the Taliban movement, Mullah Omar said: "The Taliban movement is an Afghan Taliban movement and it does not belong to any foreign country. We are Muslims who want an Islamic government in Afghanistan. Right now we haven't anything or equipment, but with the help of Allah we will keep fighting against the criminal mujahedeen. We haven't any source of money and no one is helping us."

When talk turned to him being declared Amir-ul Momineen, Mullah Omar asked the mullahs gathered before him if their intentions were good, if they were being honest with him. He said: "It is a very important title you are giving to me. Are you sure it is good? If in your heart you know it is wrong, then God will be your judge and you will not go to heaven."

With that, Mullah Omar accepted the title and took the Cloak of the Prophet from Kandahar's holiest shrine. It was the first time it had been removed from its sacred resting place since 1935, when Kandaharis took it to the city's largest Eid Gah Mosque to pray for divine intervention to stop a rampaging cholera epidemic.

Before that, it had been seen once in 1929, when Afghanistan's deposed King Amanullah had used the sacred relic to rally his Pashtun tribesmen behind him in a futile effort to regain his throne.

Amanullah and Mullah Omar couldn't have been further apart. Amanullah's reign came crashing down because he attempted to modernize Afghanistan, enroll girls in school, and discourage the use of the veil, which he ultimately banned by decree. At the peak of the campaign to unseat Amanullah, pictures were circulated in Kabul of his wife wearing Western clothes, unveiled and chatting with men. The mullahs were enraged. He was called the Kafir (Infidel) king because of his modern ways. That was in the early 1920s. Nearly seventy years later, Mullah Omar would issue his own decree making it a crime for a woman to be unveiled.

Mobs of mullahs joined with the Tajik rebel Bacha Saquo to unseat Amanullah in the late 1920s. Saquo had the support of the British colonialists, who wanted Amanullah off the throne because he had threatened to push east toward British India. Rampaging mullahs ransacked Kabul and drove Amanullah to his Pashtun home in Kandahar.

But even there the mullahs were against him. "Kafir," they would scream when they saw him. Roland Wild, a British reporter who was in Afghanistan during Amanullah's last days, described how the mullahs would rail against their deposed king in *Amanullah, Ex-King of Afghanistan* (London: 1932): "Look how he ordered you to forget the teachings of your religious masters. Remember how his ungodly queen unveiled her face and broke the rules of purdah before a foreign people."

Amanullah went to the Cloak of the Prophet to quiet their cries of "Kafir." "You call me Kafir. I will show you that in fact I am favored of Allah." With those words, he retrieved the Cloak of the Prophet and silenced their cries. They stopped calling him Kafir, but they were still too upset by his modernizing methods to help him recapture his throne. Sixty-seven years later, Mullah Omar succeeded where Amanullah had failed.

Khaksar and Omar left the Kandahar meeting together. They

drove in silence for a few moments. Khaksar wasn't sure whether to speak. But he had questions: "I asked him why he wanted to be Amir-ul Momineen, Amir of all the Muslims in the world. If it were just Afghanistan, that would have been OK, but not the world. He said it was what the ulema wanted. He didn't know that it would hurt the Taliban."

Mullah Omar's action drew no international reaction. The West had already turned Afghanistan over to the regional players, but particularly Pakistan. In the years before the Taliban captured Kabul, there was no international reflection or debate about how to encourage a more moderate Taliban.

In many distant Western capitals, the Taliban were actually seen as a good thing in that they were expected to put an end to the brutal fighting and lawlessness and bring security to a deeply insecure nation. For the West, the Taliban also represented a single entity, unlike the many factions that were destroying Kabul.

The United Nations was tasked with trying to broker a peace agreement between the Taliban and the mujahedeen government. In a bid to broker a peace agreement, the UN ignored the Taliban's treatment of women and ban on girls' education.

The UN did not challenge the Taliban when they took over Kandahar and ordered women out of work, including those women working for international organizations, among them the United Nations itself. Rather than defy the Taliban, the UN defied its own charter, which forbids host governments from dictating to the United Nations.

The Taliban were consistent, and from the very beginning, there could be no mistake about their attitude toward women. But the international community didn't care.

Rabia Bibi remembered the Taliban's takeover of Kandahar. For nearly twenty years she had worked for an international aid organization, and suddenly one day she had no job. A petite woman, standing barely five feet tall, Rabia was stubborn and feisty and the sole breadwinner for five children. She tried to defy the edict. She wanted to work. She didn't mind the Taliban's order to wear a burqa. She had always worn a burqa, that typically blue, wafting covering that would become a symbol of Taliban repression, yet had been worn in Afghanistan for generations.

Even Amir Shah, who is smart and kind and has been to New York City, wanted to know whether his wife, Habiba, could wear her burqa in New York. Habiba had worn it for more than three decades, imposed on her not by the Taliban, but first by her father and then by her husband.

The world would eventually galvanize against the burqa. But then, for Rabia Bibi it was her job that was important. She believed her international aid organization would support her. It did not.

In the same way, the UN female staff, teachers, and clerics found themselves sent home. The United Nations didn't squabble. Women's rights were not on the negotiating table between the UN and the Taliban. It was a morally weak attempt by the UN to ingratiate itself with the Taliban.

Norbert Holl, the UN special envoy, was unconcerned, even a little offended that women's rights should have the same prominence as the issue of peace. At a news conference, he said bluntly: "Women? Don't talk to me about women. I don't mention women. That is a cultural issue. I am trying to negotiate peace."

It was a remark that showed Holl's ignorance of Afghan culture. Afghans had never before outlawed women from working or girls from attending school.

In those early years of the Taliban, I often talked to Taliban commanders about their harsh edicts. In the summer of 1996, I was on the front lines with the Taliban, sipping sweet green tea from grimy glass cups with Commander Mullah Burjan in a mud bunker on the edge of Maidan Shahr, barely thirty kilometers south of Kabul. Maidan Shahr is the capital of Wardak Province but so small you can miss it if you blink. After crossing a stretch of no-man's-land at lightning speed in a little yellow taxi, with Amir Shah in the driver's seat, we found Mullah Burjan, a powerful figure who later died in battle. On that sunny summer's day, we talked above the din of outgoing rockets fired by his Taliban troops and incoming shells blasted at us from the mujahedeen positions.

I went through my questions about the fighting, the strength of their positions, and the mujahedeen government's positions. We talked for more than an hour.

As we prepared to leave, I threw out a handful of questions I often asked about the Taliban's rules concerning women. Amir Shah always winced when we got to this part of the interview, which we always did. Regardless of the Taliban we were interviewing, I liked to ask about the restrictions they imposed. It was curious to me because, as I would say to them, the wife of Islam's prophet Mohammed was a businesswoman and the Quran is full of urgings to educate both men and women.

When I asked Mullah Burjan whether the harsh restrictions that the Taliban imposed on women were more in keeping with tribal traditions and not religious injunctions, he laughed. We had had this conversation before. "Why are you always asking about women? The United Nations never mentions women to us."

It's ironic that opposition to the Taliban would eventually become almost a feminist issue with the burqa as its symbol, despite the fact that the mujahedeen government the Taliban were fighting, including many of those same leaders the United States would later return to power, were strong advocates of the burqa. Some among the mujahedeen would even refuse to talk to women.

The mujahedeen government's education minister, Younis Khalis, had publicly said education of girls was against Islam. But there had been no international outcry. In territory controlled by Ahmed Shah Massood, there had never been a girls' school, and women were rarely seen without a burqa.

The only time girls really prospered in Afghanistan was during the Communist regime, the regime that the West sought to overthrow by using the Islamic fervor of militant Muslims.

During those conversations with Taliban men like Mullah Burjan, I thought that perhaps the Taliban could have been made to understand that there were certain international standards that had to be met. They might also have come to understand the need to make concessions or perhaps might even have looked to moderates within their ranks to negotiate a middle ground. But that didn't happen.

The Taliban's Islamic fervor was quietly ignored and maybe even secretly appreciated in Western capitals, where it was seen as akin to the Islamic fervor they had used to such good effect against the Soviets. There was still no understanding of the menace spawned by the Islamic fervor they had so willfully nurtured and exploited.

Only in Pakistan was the potential of the Taliban really understood. It was a weak movement, ever more easy to manipulate as it became more isolated from other Muslim nations and ignored by the West. For Pakistan, the Taliban was an inspiring opportunity.

CHAPTER FOUR

The Moderate Taliban

The body hung at a grotesque angle. The noose must have snapped the spine because the head lolled to one side. There was something stuffed up the nose. You couldn't tell what it was unless you went right up to the swaying corpse. Then it was clear: It was money. A bill was rolled tight and shoved up into the left nostril. A partially smoked cigarette was stuck between the lifeless fingers.

The bloated and bloodied body was that of Afghanistan's former Communist president, Dr. Najibullah. I tried hard not to imagine the horrors of his last hours, terrified, ripped from the safety of a United Nations compound by Taliban men who had just taken over Kabul and wanted to avenge the deaths of friends and relatives killed when Najibullah ruled with the help of the Soviet Union.

His clothes were soaked in blood. He had been wearing the traditional *shalwar kameez,* but I couldn't be sure of the color. It looked like it might have been beige. The front of his shirt was ripped and the baggy pants were lopsided, with one leg exposed. His hands—what had been done to them? His fingers looked like they were broken. The arms hung at such an odd angle that the whole body seemed contorted.

Najibullah's remains hung from the ruins of a red and white

watchtower once used by traffic police on the road in front of the presidential palace.

Hanging next to him was his brother, Shahpur, who had been by his side throughout his rule and for the past four years inside the UN compound.

The Taliban had shoved rupee notes into Shahpur's brown suede jacket and stuffed more in his hands. He had been wearing a heavy brown shirt and jeans. I was struck by the newness of his gray running shoes.

There was no blood on Shahpur's body.

Taliban soldiers with rocket launchers strapped to their backs and Kalashnikovs strung menacingly over their shoulders hugged each other in front of Najibullah's lifeless body. Children gaped.

⁂

Najibullah and his brother had pleaded with the United Nations for help before being taken away by the Taliban. But no help came. They called the UN office in Kabul sometime around 1 A.M. on September 27, 1996, via a shortwave radio. Najibullah pleaded to the UN: "I need some security. My guards are gone. I am alone."

The mujahedeen government had already abandoned Kabul, and Najibullah's frightened guards had left with them. But before he left, the fleeing interior minister, Mohammed Fahim, who would later become the first defense minister in the post-Taliban government, offered to take Najibullah and his brother with him to the Panjshir Valley, to where the Northern Alliance was retreating.

Najibullah refused. He would stay. He was a Pashtun, like most of the Taliban, and an important man in the Ahmedzai tribe. He believed his tribal ties would save him. He had forgotten the tribal lust for revenge. Entire families have been wiped out in tribal blood feuds, and the first Pashtun men to overrun Kabul would not be deterred. Najibullah's killer was a friend of

Mullah Omar's who had lost several members of his family during the Soviet occupation of Afghanistan. He took his revenge.

But this one revenge killing was a mistake of gargantuan proportions. The Taliban would pay a heavy price. By allowing this single vicious deed, the Taliban took an irreversible step down the road to becoming an international pariah.

The UN retribution for the hanging of Najibullah was exacted by Benon Sevan, the man in charge of UN security at the time. Sevan was responsible for deciding which countries were safe for the UN to operate in and which weren't. There were varying degrees: from slightly dangerous to unacceptably dangerous. Very few countries were placed in the last category.

Sevan put the Taliban's Afghanistan on the list of unsafe countries, even though it was now safer than it had been in four years. But the decision was not a reflection on Afghanistan or Afghans: It was payback.

Sevan had guaranteed Najibullah his safety. It was Sevan who had convinced Najibullah to step down in April 1992 in favor of the mujahedeen government. For four years Sevan had shuttled between the mujahedeen and Najibullah. Although the official position of the Western world was that Najibullah should be out of power, Sevan had genuinely liked the square-shouldered Najibullah. He understood him, whereas he thought the mujahedeen leaders were radical buffoons.

In April 1992, Sevan himself went to Kabul in a small UN-owned aircraft to bring Najibullah to safety. The mujahedeen government stopped him. In fact it was a former Communist, General Momin, who had switched sides to join the mujahedeen, who controlled the airport and refused to let Najibullah leave. Just as Najibullah was ready to board the UN aircraft, he was ordered back to Kabul.

Sevan argued, but in vain. Finally, he took Najibullah to the UN compound where he would live for the next four years, watching from his sanctuary as the warring factions that made up the mujahedeen government destroyed his capital.

Sevan's security rating of the Taliban's Afghanistan meant that only a handful of UN staff could be in country at any one time and all the UN's Afghan operations were headquartered in neighboring Pakistan. It helped to further isolate and condemn, from afar, the Taliban.

The UN refused to give the Taliban Afghanistan's seat at the United Nations or even leave it vacant. Instead, the UN chose to recognize former president Burhanuddin Rabbani as the rightful head of Afghanistan's government and left the UN seat with him. It didn't matter that Rabbani controlled only small slivers of the country or that Kabul was littered with the victims of his four-year rule.

Many of the mujahedeen's atrocities—seven-year-old Maryam, whose throat had been slit, the rape and scalping of Ghulam Jan's wife and the wives of his friends—had been committed by Sayyaf's men when he was Rabbani's deputy prime minister. I once asked Rabbani about the atrocities that his men and Sayyaf's men had committed when they ruled Kabul. He tersely called them a "mistake." Nonetheless, the UN afforded him official recognition as lawful president of Afghanistan.

With Najibullah's hanging, the battle lines were drawn: The United Nations and the international community were on one side, and the Taliban on the other. No middle ground was left open to strengthen the voices of the moderate men within the Taliban's central command. It cut them off at the knees. Mohammed Khaksar was one of many who felt abandoned:

> In the very first place I blame the international community, because at the very beginning when it began its talks with the Taliban, there was no sign of flexibility. The tone was harsh, the attitude was demanding. There was no give-and-take. When we talked to the United Nations before the Taliban took Kabul there was flexibility. There were negotiations. But later there was nothing, no flexibility. Their talk was very tough.

After outright refusing to talk to the Taliban about their treatment of women before they seized Kabul, the UN suddenly acted outraged by their behavior. Afghanistan became a feminist cause championed by the largely male UN. It was pure vindictiveness. The inconsistency was blatant, when one compared the new cause to UN policy toward such Arab nations as Saudi Arabia, where women must be completely veiled and some are forced to wear leather facial coverings that look like a muzzle, where women can't drive or travel anywhere unaccompanied by a man.

Within Afghanistan, the Taliban had disarmed the warlords and made even the remotest roads secure, forcing the Northern Alliance into a tiny enclave.

The Taliban had wiped out Afghanistan's production of poppies, which supply the international trade in heroin. Afghanistan became the first country in the entire world to get rid of its narcotics trade in a single year, without any deaths. Afghanistan went from producing more than 4,000 tons of opium to zero. The United Nations, Washington, and just about everyone else dismissed the ban by saying the Taliban imposed it to drive up the price of opium so it could cash in on the large stockpiles it possessed. In truth, the UN drug agency at the time said there was no evidence to prove the Taliban were wholesale stockpilers, but even if it were true, it doesn't explain how the Taliban managed to accomplish the ban. The stockpiles would benefit only a few, yet the Taliban forced hundreds of thousands of poor small farmers from across the country to stop growing the crop. Hundreds of thousands of day laborers lost their livelihood because of the ban.

The same year the Taliban got rid of its poppies, the UN, ignoring the pleas of its representatives in Pakistan, ended its aid to the now cropless farmers, because, it said, it didn't want to give the religious militia recognition. The Taliban moderates even suggested a commission be set up that would be made up of UN representatives and Taliban, in a 50–50 split. This commission would decide how aid money would be spent, allowing the UN to monitor the allocation of aid and at the same time strengthening the stature of the moderates within the Taliban. The UN again refused.

The moderate Taliban foreign minister, Wakil Ahmed Muttawakil, tried to negotiate a compromise, to find common ground, a means by which the United Nations could keep its distance but still alleviate the chronic poverty in Afghanistan as well as bolster the more moderate voices within the Taliban central command.

Khaksar spoke for many when he said:

"Fine. Don't accept us as the government, but come and help us with the reconstruction." But no. The United Nations wouldn't come. It had to be all or nothing. There were those of us who tried to find alternatives, tried to find ways to slowly, step by step, make things better. But there was no flexibility from the international community, and what did it get from this? It got nothing. Afghanistan got nothing. The Afghan people got nothing, and we couldn't do anything about the foreign fighters until it was too late. But I know if there had been some flexibility, there were people in the Taliban who wanted to work with the international community, who didn't want the foreign fighters, who wanted them gone. But with no help from outside we couldn't do anything, and then it was too late.

The moderate men of the Taliban were soon alone and frightened into silence. The Taliban's circle of friends kept shrinking until by 1999, it included scarcely more than Pakistan, Saudi Arabia, the United Arab Emirates, and al Qaeda. By then Mullah Omar had become convinced that no matter what the Taliban did, the fear and loathing the Taliban engendered in the West would never be satisfied.

There is one truism in Afghanistan: Strength equals respect, weakness equals fear.

There were ordinary Afghans who opposed Mullah Omar's

Taliban. Khudaidad, the mullah from Khost, said Mullah Omar got his strength from the fact that everyone knew he had foreign help: "I, along with thousands of other mullahs in Afghanistan, we all knew from the first days of jihad that no one can make himself a leader without foreign help or assistance. People, including mullahs, were afraid of Mullah Omar, but no one was a match for him. He had help from Pakistan, Saudi Arabia, and the United Arab Emirates."

Khaksar had also talked to disgruntled Taliban:

> If there were 100 men who wanted to see a change, then behind them would be 1,000, but they were afraid and who would help them? Who would help their families if the Taliban arrested them? They were afraid. The world was angry with the Taliban. The world didn't want to find a way to work with anyone in the Taliban, no matter who they were. We knew that and we knew that we couldn't protect anyone who wanted to work with us. We couldn't say there was help there, because there wasn't. There was no one.

The moderate men of the Taliban were perceived as weak; they had no power behind them. Mullah Omar, on the other hand, had Pakistan, bin Laden, and a growing militia of foreign fighters.

This Afghan respect for strength was also once explained to me by Hamid Karzai, a friend of sixteen years, long before he could have dreamed of becoming president of Afghanistan.

Karzai was always a moderate man. His father was a tribal elder from Kandahar, home of many of the Taliban. Hamid had even supported the Taliban when they first emerged because he, too, wanted the warlords kicked out and saw no future for his country under the lawless mujahedeen government. Although Hamid had been a deputy foreign minister in the mujahedeen government, he had to flee for his life after he found himself caught between feuding warlords.

At first, Karzai tried to justify the Taliban: "You don't understand, Kathy. They are mullahs who want to stop the killing and the stealing and the raping by these mujahedeen commanders. They don't want power." At one point he was even asked by the Taliban to be their representative at the United Nations. Hamid seemed ready to take the posting, but he said that Pakistan had intervened to oppose him.

When the 9/11 attacks occurred, Hamid was living in Pakistan's southwestern city of Quetta, a dusty, always dirty city of noisy bazaars, black-exhaust belching rickshaws and buses, and rugged tribesmen. It was a stone's throw from the Afghan border. Days earlier, the government of Pakistan had refused to extend Hamid's visa. They were going to throw him out.

He always had hopes for Afghanistan, and when the United States declared war on the Taliban in October 2001, after many discussions with his tribesmen, Hamid decided to go to Afghanistan to try to rally his southern Pashtun tribesmen there around his leadership. For years he had been meeting secretly with them. But he was alone. At that point he didn't have U.S. backing, which had been granted to a friend of Karzai's, Abdul Haq, a former mujahedeen commander who went into Afghanistan after September 11, was discovered by Arab fighters, shot dozens of times, and hanged.

On his trip to Afghanistan, Hamid was accompanied only by a small number of close friends. The tribesmen asked Hamid who was backing him. Were the Americans helping him? "When I told them I was on my own, they were afraid. They said they couldn't fight the Taliban alone."

Even on the eve of the U.S.-led assault on Afghanistan, Afghans weren't ready publicly to support anyone who couldn't prove he had powerful allies. Afghans are honest people, Hamid likes to say. And they were honest with him. "They just told me that they didn't think I could win against the Taliban on my own and they couldn't risk being with me when I lost." It was the Afghan truism writ large: Strength succeeds.

And it was always the weakest who suffered most—whether from the depredations of their own government or from the stubborn refusal of the international community to engage in their ordinary suffering. I remember encountering a particularly wretched and stooped old man in November 2000 in eastern Nangarhar Province. His gray beard was caked with dust. The heat was stifling, the wind painfully dry. The old man was throwing shovel after shovel of dirt onto the road, hoping passing motorists, who kicked up the dirt as they roared past, would throw a few Afghani notes out the windows of their vehicles. He leaned on his splintered shovel when he spoke. His eyes were deeply bloodshot from the dust. A year earlier he had been a day laborer, working in the poppy fields, earning about $30 a month. His voice was shaky, and as he talked, he suddenly just stopped and cried. It was such a soft sound, almost as if he didn't want us to hear. His head slumped forward. The weight of his sad world just seemed to sit right on his shoulders. He cursed the Taliban, the United Nations, the world. His curses were barely audible, as if he just had no more strength to issue them.

November would have been the peak of the poppy-planting season during the years of mujahedeen rule. The rocky roads wound through village after village of eastern Nangarhar, each smaller and poorer than the last. Homes were made of mud, and even the smallest house was encased in the traditional high wall that hid the women inside. The practice of hiding their women inside was an ancient one in poor Afghanistan.

For centuries most farmers had grown poppies. Occasionally, a farmer might try wheat, but it just didn't bring in the same revenue. The April opium harvests brought great rewards to the busy day laborers. They would run their sharp blade down the side of the poppy bulb to release the milky white liquid that became opium when dried. Farmers didn't have to worry about getting their opium to market because the market came to them, or rather, the middleman who trekked from farm to farm collecting opium, bartered the price, paid the farmer, and moved to the next farm.

Opium was the only collateral farmers could use to get loans to buy next year's seeds, as well as a winter supply of staples like sugar, tea, and cooking oil. That's why the total observance of the Taliban ban was so extraordinary: They had uprooted a centuries-old lifestyle and economy. Sher Gul, the elder of Mimla village in Nangahar, tried, over a cup of green tea, to explain why they were not growing poppies. There were a couple of reasons, but the biggest seemed to be that the Taliban understood how the village dynamics worked and used it to make sure their ban was enforced.

Gul explained patiently: "First the Taliban sent a message to every village. It was pretty clear. The Taliban said that wherever poppies were found growing, both the village elder and the mullah would be arrested, along with the farmer, and jailed for one month. The farmer would also be charged the cost of destroying his poppy crop."

Not long after that announcement, there was a story in the area of one farmer who vowed to defy the order. The Taliban arrested him, and then to add insult to injury, blackened his face to humiliate him and paraded him throughout his village on the back of a truck. The Taliban frightened both the village elder and the mullah into action.

Sher Gul had been a poppy farmer himself, like his father before him. He was unhappy about the ban, but he certainly wasn't considering defying it.

His massive frame strained the small bed of rope on which we sat. He wasn't a rich man, and like so many other poppy farmers, he was deeply in debt. He owed $850. His home was a cluster of small cement buildings reached by crossing a rickety old wooden bridge that spanned a whimpering brook almost dried up from years of drought. Children surrounded him. I couldn't be sure how many were his. He told me several of his family members lived together on the compound.

To help him enforce the ban, Sher Gul recruited several villagers, his own poppy posse that would patrol the fields. The patrols started early, just as the sun was peeking over the horizon and the fields were still a little dewy. He explained:

You see the best time to plant the poppy seeds is just at sunrise when the air is cool and the earth is slightly damp from the night. It is very good then. We know that this is when people will try to plant, so we go from farm to farm on horseback. When we find someone planting poppies, right away we stop them. We make them stop planting. In the mosque, the mullah also tells them not to plant. We know the Taliban will put us in jail and not just the farmer. Before, when the mujahedeen were in the government, we could bribe the commander, who would make sure that the village chief, like me, got something and that the local police chief got something. But now there is no local commander, and the police chief knows the Taliban will punish him if a village is growing poppies, so then all of us would be in jail. We know that the Taliban are not joking.

Opium production, in this way, was choked off. Yet the Taliban received not a flicker of acknowledgment or credit, even though they had achieved almost instantly what a ten-year campaign and billions of U.S. dollars had failed to do in Colombia.

※

In 1999, the United States turned down what was probably the last best offer by Mohammed Khaksar to galvanize the moderates within the Taliban and try to unseat the hard-liners and rid Afghanistan of Osama bin Laden.

From his shabby wallet, Khaksar gently pulled out a carefully folded letter, half of a tattered five-rupee note, and two business cards and offered them as evidence of his secret 1999 meeting with two representatives of the U.S. Consulate in Peshawar in neighboring Pakistan.

It was a dangerous assignation. The Taliban's intelligence was good, but bin Laden's was even better. Khaksar had to be careful because to be discovered would have meant certain death.

Khaksar met two men. One was Peter McIllwain, the CIA chief in Pakistan's northwest frontier city of Peshawar, who was fully aware of Khaksar's position and influence within the Taliban and knew that he had access to Taliban leaders, to the command council, and to foreign fighters.

Khaksar had been a true believer in the Taliban's mission at first. He had not been an opportunist. He saw Islam as the way to end the factional fighting that had turned his country into an anarchic collection of fiefdoms ruled by warlords. But five years later, Khaksar had become disillusioned enough to look to the Americans for help.

Khaksar was a desperate man. He hadn't wanted to turn to outsiders. He had first tried to rally like-minded mullahs to resist. But they were afraid. What could he do for them if the Taliban discovered their resistance? He needed powerful friends to rival Pakistan, al Qaeda, and several Arab countries. He reflected: "The Pakistanis and the Arabs built mosques, talked about all Muslims everywhere coming together. It wasn't Afghanistan anymore. My thinking was that they would destroy my country."

He hooked up with the Americans through two men he called "low-level commanders with the Taliban." They had befriended him, talked politics. He had been careful and listened. They shared their disillusionment and offered to introduce him to the Americans. A cautious man, Khaksar checked their credentials, and "eventually I understood they were businessmen who thought they could make money if they brought an important Taliban to the Americans." Khaksar didn't care about their motives. Their greed was in some ways reassuring.

In April 1999, Khaksar knew the strength bin Laden wielded over the Taliban and saw that his homeland was being used. There were no specific early signs warning of the attacks against the United States, but Khaksar believed bin Laden had lied when, in 1998, he had promised Mullah Omar he wouldn't use Afghan soil to plot attacks against others.

Khaksar also knew Pakistan was interfering. Pakistan had taken bin Laden in and hidden him for several weeks after the August 1998 attack by the United States, when more than seventy Tomahawk cruise missiles blasted terrorist training camps in eastern Afghanistan. The target had been bin Laden.

Dozens of four-by-four trucks took bin Laden and a small army of Arab fighters to a Pakistani army commando training camp at Chirat in northwest Pakistan. After the attack, the United States had told the Taliban to get rid of bin Laden. Mullah Omar claimed not to know where he had gone. In fact, Mullah Omar, Pakistan, and bin Laden had carried out an elaborate game of hide-and-seek to keep the United States off guard, pretending bin Laden was missing while hiding him in Pakistan.

Khaksar disguised the reasons for his meeting with the CIA in Pakistan, telling the Taliban he needed medical tests in Islamabad: "I knew someone would try to make trouble for me so I made arrangements to go to the hospital." After checking himself out of the hospital, he called the Taliban's prime minister to let him know he would be spending a few more days in Pakistan. He didn't want anyone wondering where he was, looking for him. He was a careful man.

Khaksar was first brought to an American teacher at a Christian school. Khaksar and the teacher talked for hours, mostly about religion. Khaksar said the teacher wanted to explore the Taliban's beliefs. Eventually, the conversation turned to politics.

The teacher told Khaksar he wasn't the man to talk politics. He said Khaksar should go the next day to the U.S. Consulate and tell them an American doctor sent him.

At nine the next morning, he went to the home of Gregory Marchese, vice consul at the U.S. Consulate. McIllwain was there.

Speaking through an interpreter, McIllwain had questions for Khaksar:

"What do you want from us? What do you know about Osama bin Laden? What can you give us on bin Laden's whereabouts?" I told him: "Really what I am afraid of is that these Arabs have connections to outside countries, lots of connections, and one day they will do something in the world, and everything will be on the head of Afghanistan." I told them that you can't defeat the Taliban militarily. They are too strong, but politically you can defeat them. I told them it is not the work you can do in one day or two days. I want to make this a big program so that if something happens to me, if I get killed there are other people who would continue. I told them it could be done. I told them that I couldn't do it alone. That no one would follow me if I was alone.

As the Taliban's deputy interior minister, Khaksar had thousands of policemen under his command and had links to intelligence sources within the Taliban. His network was solid. But he needed the United States behind him to convince others to work with him and against Mullah Omar.

The Americans promised to take his offer to Washington. Before the meeting ended, McIllwain ripped a five-rupee note in half. Khaksar was given half and the Americans kept the other. Neither side wanted to be betrayed. Khaksar told McIllwain: "If anyone comes to you and says they represent me, ask for my half of the five-rupee note. If he doesn't have it, he is a fake."

Khaksar returned to Afghanistan. He heard only once from the two Americans. They rejected his offer. They wrote him a letter in Pashtu. He has kept the letter, although it is now tattered. But it is still legible. I had it translated.

In hindsight it was particularly confusing. The CIA said the mujahedeen it had backed during the 1980s had turned against them. The CIA told Khaksar it was afraid of making the same mistake by backing him. Khaksar didn't understand.

He was offering to organize Afghans to rid his homeland of the foreign fighters, who were attacking the United States. He wasn't offering to reorganize the mujahedeen that the CIA had backed during the 1980s.

The letter, awkwardly translated, reads: "We don't want to make the mistakes like we made in the holy war. We gave much help and it later went against us . . . But my boss is interested."

What the CIA was interested in, it transpired, was getting bin Laden, but without becoming involved, holding out instead the enticement of $5 million, the reward at the time for bin Laden.

The CIA missed the chance. Khaksar knew there were men among the Taliban who wanted a change; he knew there were some within the Northern Alliance who could be approached. He had already made secret contact with Ahmed Shah Massood. He was ready to try to end the fighting and evict the foreign fighters.

He summarized the dilemma:

I was waiting for a program from the Americans, a program to defeat the Taliban and a program to hand over bin Laden. Then bin Laden's security was not so tight; there was more facility to get him.

But people were not crazy to kill bin Laden if they could not be guaranteed support. What would happen to their families if they were killed? How could they attack the Taliban and the foreign fighters without some help from outside?

What was this $5 million? And who could believe that they would get it, and what if you died before you could collect it? What then? For sure, your family would be killed. Who would look after your family, who would protect them? Right away someone would capture your family. They didn't understand.

For me, it wasn't for bin Laden that I wanted a program, that was what it was for the Americans, but for me it was for my country.

So, yet again, Afghanistan got nothing. Nor did America. In 1999, the only apparent winner was the unopposed Osama bin Laden.

CHAPTER FIVE

The Taliban Bloodied

It was a painfully hot May weekend in 1997 when Taliban tanks flying the white flag of the religious army rumbled into Afghanistan's ancient northern city of Mazar-e-Sharif.

Bearded men in turbans packed into black pickup trucks bristling with antiaircraft guns and rocket launchers shouted "God is great" as they roared through the rutted main street. They ripped giant posters of the burly Uzbek warlord Rashid Dostum from traffic posts, pillars, and public buildings.

Hours earlier, Dostum had slipped into neighboring Uzbekistan across the yawning steel bridge that spanned the Oxus River with a suitcase full of money under his arm and a couple of generals at his side.

The Uzbek government ordered its border sealed. The steel girders of the bridge were quickly encased in coils of barbed wire. Tanks drove onto the bridge and stopped in a defiant stance, their gun barrels aimed into Afghanistan.

For the previous few weeks, Uzbekistan's totalitarian president, Islam Karimov, had watched nervously as the Taliban marched through northern Afghanistan. He worried their successes would inflame the creeping Islamic insurgency in his own country.

Dostum's hold on the gas-rich northern third of Afghanistan

had begun to slip months earlier after his ally Abdul Malik defected to the Taliban and took with him the loyalty of ethnic Uzbeks who were the backbone of Dostum's army. Dostum had been a cruel commander: Whatever loyalty he inspired was rooted in fear.

Stories abounded of Dostum's cruelty. He was said to have buried live officers who challenged his authority and to have kidnapped and raped the wives of mutinous officers. Dostum's men had terrorized villages, skulking around by night, raiding and robbing homes. People were too afraid to complain.

Dostum had cut a fearsome figure in his 150-year-old walled redoubt outside Shebergan, the capital of his home province of Jozjan. It was called Qali-e-Jhangi, or Fortress of War. I had been there several times during the mujahedeen's rule. Its rooms were ornate, surrounded by balustrades and guarded by hulking ethnic Uzbek men who looked visibly shaken each time Dostum walked into the room.

Malik had broken ranks with Dostum and forged an alliance with the Taliban to avenge the killing of Abdur Rahman Pahlawan, the chief of his Pahlawan tribe, the largest of northwestern Faryab Province, which was a rich canvas of orchards and rolling hills.

Dostum had ordered Abdur Rahman Pahlawan's execution to cauterize the tribe's growing influence in the north. The killing was carried out in tribal fashion. Although the chief was suspicious, he accepted an invitation to dinner with Dostum, thinking he would be safe because tribal etiquette doesn't allow anyone to kill a guest.

The dinner party bristled with armed men. After the two men had finished their meal, Dostum politely and formally walked the chief to his car. Then he ordered him killed.

Malik's mutiny offered the Taliban an alliance that would give them control of the northern third of the country, everything except the Panjshir Valley.

Malik didn't have much in common with the Taliban. He wasn't a religious man; he liked his alcohol, his music, and his television. When I first met him, he patted his clean-shaven face and ruefully observed that he would have to begin growing a beard, a Taliban requirement.

Malik's defection added to the Taliban's confidence in their unchallenged supremacy. Kabul had fallen to them eight months earlier, and since their beginning in 1994, the Taliban had not experienced a single setback in their takeover of Afghanistan. Now the north seemed to have been handed to them.

Mazar-e-Sharif is an ancient northern citadel at the edge of a vast arid plain that ends at the Oxus River and Afghanistan's northern border with the Central Asian states. The blue-tiled minarets of the domed Shrine of Hazrat Ali dominate Mazar-e-Sharif's skyline. Dozens of gray and white pigeons fly constantly above the dome. Legend has it that only the white pigeons land within the fenced grounds of the shrine.

Dostum chose to make his last stand in Mazar-e-Sharif and still-loyal Uzbeks provided him with his forces. On May 22, when I arrived there, it seemed that the battle for Mazar-e-Sharif could go either way. Although Dostum's soldiers had conceded large parts of his northern empire to the Taliban, they had amassed in strength to defend Mazar-e-Sharif and his fortress headquarters in neighboring Jozjan.

Soon after I arrived, the pudgy General Yousuf gave a military briefing at the fortress. Yousuf's rotund body quivered with rage as he outlined the Taliban's likely assault. I questioned Yousuf's strategy to defeat the Taliban, saying they seemed unstoppable.

He avoided my question. I tried a few more times to find out how he expected to stop them, but the briefing ended without an answer. Before I left, Yousuf accused me of suggesting the Taliban could defeat Dostum's army and ordered me to leave Mazar-e-Sharif. When I asked him how, since all the flights were full, he barked, "I don't care how you leave, but I want you out of Mazar-e-Sharif. I don't care if you have to walk out through Uzbekistan."

For the next two days, while I wondered what to do, Yousuf and Dostum were quietly preparing to quit. By the time the Taliban, led by Malik's mutinous Uzbek soldiers, had entered the city, both Yousuf and Dostum were heading for Uzbekistan on foot.

The Taliban celebrated their victory with prayers at the magnificent shrine. Malik moved into the palatial governor's residence, which was outfitted with deep red carpets and heavy wooden furniture. There he waited for the Taliban to appoint him governor of all of northern Afghanistan as reward for his allegiance.

Events moved quickly. The Taliban ordered thousands of fresh troops to Mazar-e-Sharif. The dilapidated airport on the outskirts of the city saw a constant traffic of cargo aircraft dropping them off.

Living in a liberal city compared to others in Afghanistan, the residents of Mazar-e-Sharif wondered what restrictions the Taliban would impose. They had heard of the strict religious edicts issued in Kabul.

Mazar-e-Sharif had escaped the 1980s anti-Soviet war in Afghanistan untouched. Barely a one-hour drive from the border with Uzbekistan, Mazar-e-Sharif had spent the war years occupied uncontested by Soviet soldiers and controlled throughout by Dostum, who then held the rank of general in Afghanistan's Communist government.

The Taliban wasted no time imposing their rigid rule, targeting women first. They ordered women off the job, demanded they wear the fully covering burqa and stay home, unless accompanied by men. Movie theaters and music shops were closed.

In less than twenty-four hours, the city had begun visibly to fill up with Taliban soldiers. They started ripping apart music cassettes, festooning pillars with the ruined tapes; they ripped posters advertising Indian films from movie theater walls; they shut down the women's university.

A feeling of foreboding was in the air already, especially in the poorer Hazara Shiite neighborhoods. Men were angry, and they had begun to hide their weapons from the Taliban, hoping that they would be able to hand them to their own mujahedeen fighters, the Hezb-e-Wahadat, whom they were praying would return to retake the city.

The next day, Pakistan sent a representative to Mazar-e-Sharif to congratulate the Taliban on their victory and to officially recognize the religious movement as the government of Afghanistan. Saudi Arabia and the United Arab Emirates became the only other countries to give recognition to the Taliban.

I watched Pakistan's envoy, Aziz Khan, a gray-haired career diplomat, pump the hand of the Taliban's foreign minister, Mullah Ghous, a heavyset Pashtun from Kandahar whose eyes were sensitive to light and who always wore dark glasses. Ghous had arrived in Mazar-e-Sharif with the Taliban reinforcements to consolidate the takeover of the area.

Yet the alliance with Malik seemed to be faltering. The Taliban had appointed someone else, a Kandahari, to take control of the north and had offered Malik limited local authority as governor of Mazar-e-Sharif.

Malik wasn't happy, and there were already reports of sporadic firefights between Malik's men and Taliban soldiers. It was almost dusk when Mullah Ghous and Aziz Khan held a self-congratulatory news conference to celebrate the capture of Mazar-e-Sharif. The last time I saw Mullah Ghous, he was giving Aziz a bear hug. He fled south soon after.

Within twenty-four hours of their arrival in Mazar-e-Sharif, the young Taliban troops had been lured into a trap of Malik's invention. His men quietly let the Shiite mujahedeen back into the city to rearm. Then, when the Taliban moved into the Shiite neighborhood to quell the uprising, thinking that Malik's troops were supporting their rear, they found themselves in a classic ambush, pinned in winding streets whose exits they did not know and could not find.

They saw the minarets of Hazrat Ali's shrine in the distance, but they couldn't get to them. At every turn they were attacked; they fled down dead-end streets, they battered at gates that wouldn't open. They were trapped. Malik's men had sealed their exit. They had nowhere to run, and the heavily armed Shiite Muslims, who reviled the Taliban, launched a ferocious attack.

Hundreds of Taliban were slaughtered. Using the rusted bayonets of their Kalashnikov rifles, Shiite Muslim fighters mutilated the bodies of the dead. They gouged out their eyes, cut off their noses, and lacerated their corpses. The Taliban had to abandon their dead where they fell as the battle raged for more than sixteen hours.

Soon the two sides were exchanging rocket fire. Hour after hour was punctuated by pounding explosions and endless small-arms fire. When it was over, hundreds of Taliban were dead and 2,000 had been taken prisoner. As the Red Cross was looking for volunteers to pick up the dead, Shiite Muslims were still mutilating bodies. I came across one man waving a knife dripping with blood and shouting: "This is what we do to outsiders."

I saw hundreds of Taliban prisoners stuffed inside the back of trucks. They would all be killed. An Uzbek guard, who had taken them prisoner, later said they were driven to the plains north of Mazar-e-Sharif, where they were slaughtered.

He explained how he killed them. First he forced them at gunpoint to jump into deep wells and then he lined up his men, who then fired their Kalashnikovs into the wells before tossing in grenades. His men alone were responsible for killing 1,500 Taliban prisoners.

The Taliban asked the United Nations to investigate the carnage but it made only one attempt. It acknowledged that massive killings had occurred but never followed up.

The defeat of Mazar-e-Sharif was the Taliban's first loss, and it had been brutal. It was a defining moment for the religious movement.

The massacre at Mazar-e-Sharif brought to a brutal end an amazing string of victories that had given the Taliban an almost effortless control over most of the country. Before Mazar-e-Sharif, it had seemed the Taliban were invulnerable. Even their enemies had begun to think they were invincible, unstoppable.

But the catastrophic loss of Mazar-e-Sharif destroyed the Taliban myth of invincibility. One consequence was to transform a government already isolated by the international community into a paranoid regime, insecure and vulnerable to the blandishments of the Arabs and to the jihadis, who were controlled by Pakistan.

The Taliban's rigid interpretation of Islam reflected their uneducated tribal roots more than it demonstrated a coherent religious observation. But the starkness of their creed, its apparent purity and authenticity, coupled with the sense that they were victims of the West, became a valuable commodity to both Pakistan and bin Laden.

Bin Laden used the Taliban to entice new recruits to al Qaeda and to his battle against the West. He presented the example of the Taliban as a pure Islamic regime that was loathed by the West because of the purity of its devotion. The Taliban could not have been better tools if he had fashioned them himself.

The more isolated the Taliban became, the more bin Laden molded them into his likeness, which reflected his own repressive Wahabi beliefs, widespread in his home of Saudi Arabia. The Saudi practice of violent public punishments would, after the middle of 1997, become a hallmark of the Taliban regime and clearly showed the Saudi influence over it.

Even when the mujahedeen government ruled Afghanistan there were public executions, but under the Taliban the executions were given the same weekly schedule as in Saudi Arabia. Even today in Saudi Arabia, the guilty are beheaded every Friday in the town squares. Their trials are closed. The laws of evidence are secret. Yet despite the violence of their punishments, Saudi Arabia has escaped the Western hysteria that has been directed at the Taliban.

A witness to one beheading in Saudi Arabia told me the executioner slices the head clean off and then a doctor reattaches the head for burial. Both men and women are beheaded. Once, an entire Pakistani family was to be beheaded on drug-related charges until a human rights group intervened and forced the Pakistani embassy to intervene and save the children.

Closed trials thus became a feature of the Taliban government. The Saudi practice of an eye for an eye and the literal interpretation of the Quran became another hallmark. It included cutting off hands as punishment for theft.

The defeat at Mazar-e-Sharif hit at the very heart of the Taliban movement, because it angered the Pashtun tribesmen of the south who were its backbone. They wanted to know where their sons were, when would they return. Mullah Omar had no answers for them.

In those first months after the Mazar-e-Sharif defeat, no one knew where the missing Taliban were. It was known only that 2,000 Taliban, many of them young boys, were seen being hauled off to a prison. The slaughter was discovered much later.

The UN left Mazar-e-Sharif as soon as the firing stopped and evacuated its staff to Uzbekistan within days of the Taliban defeat, fearing a retaliatory strike.

In conservative Afghanistan, and particularly in Pashtun traditions, families are closely linked; cousins marry cousins, and brothers marry their brother's widow to care for the children. After the Mazar-e-Sharif defeat, families waited to hear about their children; young brides about their husbands, children about their fathers.

Mullah Omar sought the help of the United Nations but got only the cursory probe and an admission that it looked as though the Taliban had been massacred. But nothing else was done; no detailed investigations, no forensic tests, no outcry. Mullah Omar's resentment of the West deepened.

Recruitment into the Taliban ranks also became more difficult. Taliban fighters heard horror stories of the massacres, of the torture and humiliation. They were terrified to be sent to northern Afghanistan, and within the rank and file there was a growing sense that the world didn't care about them. A commander I knew from central Ghazni Province told me at the time: "I am hiding from Mullah Omar because I don't want to go to the north. We know they can do anything to us and no one will do anything. No one cares about the Taliban."

When the Taliban returned to Mazar-e-Sharif one year later, they carried out their own brutal massacre of Shiite Muslims. That did cause outrage, and the United Nations subsequently launched investigations.

In the meantime, Mullah Omar, finding it difficult to get new recruits, looked elsewhere for fighters and found willing Arab warriors. They brought him even closer to bin Laden, whose money financed new weapons and, even more important, paid Afghan conscripts.

When the international noose tightened around the Taliban in 1998 with the first round of UN-imposed sanctions and the failed August attempt by the United States to kill bin Laden in eastern Afghanistan with Tomahawk cruise missiles, the pressure on Mullah Omar became intense. Until then he had willingly used bin Laden's money and enlisted his Arab fighters on his front lines, but he had paid little attention to the increasingly large number of foreign forces gathering in Afghanistan. Western hysteria claimed the Taliban were the architects of the terrorist training camps. In fact, they had been a feature of Afghanistan since the 1980s. The mujahedeen government, which was later embraced by the United States, had given sanctuary to Arab militants wanted by their home governments, had allowed terrorist training camps to be operated by both Arabs and Pakistanis, and had refused to hand over Aymen al-Zawahri to Egypt even after he was convicted in absentia of the assassination of Anwar Sadat.

During the mujahedeen government, there were terrorist training camps in eastern Nangarhar Province, in Kunar, Laghman, Logar, and Paktia Provinces. Thousands of young men were training. But under the Taliban, the numbers in these camps mushroomed. I was told that by 1998, there were upward of 20,000 foreign fighters in Afghanistan. Most of the fighters came from Middle Eastern countries, but there were others from Chechnya, Uzbekistan, Tajikistan, Indonesia, China, Britain, and even some from the United States.

Mullah Omar got involved in the training camps after the 1998 UN sanctions and attacks by the United States. By then he was hardened against the West.

Omar amalgamated the largest camps that trained foreign fighters and ordered them into one camp at Rishkore on the outskirts of Kabul. During Taliban rule, any unauthorized visitor caught even in the vicinity of Rishkore was jailed. Rishkore covered several acres. It was subdivided into nationalities, with each nationality having its own commander. The Pakistanis were commanded by Harakat-e-Islami and Jaish-e-Mohammed, two organizations that became deeply entwined in the Taliban movement. Juman Namangani, who was later killed in the U.S. bombing of Afghanistan, commanded the Chechens and Uzbeks.

From Rishkore, foreign fighters were sent by the truckload north of Kabul to fight the Northern Alliance. On the front lines, Taliban commanders talked admiringly of their fighting spirit. One Taliban said: "They don't care if they die. They will stay and fight. If the fighting is really bad, we sometimes escape and they stay and fight. When it is over we return."

Mullah Omar put the foreign fighters directly under his control and under the control of the defense and intelligence ministries. He ordered bin Laden to stop paying money directly to Taliban commanders or ministers. The defense and intelligence ministries by now dominated the Taliban central command. Mullah Omar was spending more time with bin Laden.

Bin Laden had begun construction of a massive mosque and religious school in southern Kandahar. In 2000, he built Mullah Omar a fortress after a powerful truck bomb exploded outside his Kandahar home, killing more than forty people, including several of his guards. No one knew who did it. Iran was suspected because the Taliban had killed their diplomats in Mazar-e-Sharif earlier, but other Taliban were suspected as well, Taliban fed up with the regime. Suspicion also fell on tribesmen whose sons had never returned from Mazar-e-Sharif in 1997.

By the time he moved into his bunker, Mullah Omar had become a full-blown paranoid despot. He met few people. In January 2002, I went through the ruins of his house after the collapse of the Taliban, and I thought then that perhaps he had had premonitions of what was to come. Bin Laden, whose Saudi family fortune was made in the construction business, built an underground bunker in Mullah Omar's home that could withstand the most powerful of explosions.

The bunker had been built beneath concrete and massive amounts of rubber designed to cushion any explosions. It worked. When the Taliban fled after the U.S. bombing, the bunker was intact. Still hanging—it seemed almost with a hint of defiance—was a small crystal chandelier over Mullah Omar's single bed. Not even a single piece of glass was broken. I imagined him lying in his simple wooden bed on the thin mattress, listening to the planes overhead, the pounding of the bombs, the rattle of his chandelier—what a weirdly incongruous image.

In December 2000, the UN imposed a second round of sanctions on Afghanistan. By then bin Laden and al Qaeda were financing the defense and intelligence ministries, and bin Laden himself held the job of deputy defense minister.

Al Qaeda and Pakistan, through the jihadis of Jaish-e-Mohammed and Harakat-e-Islami, took over responsibility for providing the backbone of the Taliban's military operations in Afghanistan.

Arab and Pakistani fighters composed entire divisions. They were deployed to the Shomali Plains north of Kabul and to Bamiyan, where Hazara Shiite Muslims dominated. Taliban and Arab fighters in Bamiyan conducted violent battles, and Hazaras who resisted were killed.

Bin Laden eventually orchestrated the destruction of Bamiyan's famous statues of Buddha, those ancient monuments hewn from the sandstone mountain face, carved in the third and fifth centuries A.D. when Buddhism flourished in Afghanistan. Tucked inside the mountain beside the largest of the statues was a staircase that stopped at intervals where Buddhist monks once worshiped.

Bin Laden's Wahabi faith reviled the statues. The destruction of the statues provides one of the most significant pieces of evidence of bin Laden's total control over the Taliban. It drove an irreparable wedge between the Taliban and the rest of the world. And it ensured the Taliban belonged exclusively to al Qaeda and Pakistan.

Left to himself, Mullah Omar would not have threatened the statues. In fact, he called them a national treasure and suggested that they might be a source of income. In late 1999, just sixteen months before they were destroyed, Mullah Omar ordered them protected. The edict he issued read:

> Any excavation or trading in cultural heritage objects is strongly forbidden and will be punished in accordance with the law. The famous Buddhist statues at Bamiyan were made before the event of Islam in Afghanistan, and are amongst the largest of the kind in Afghanistan and in the world. In Afghanistan there are no Buddhists to worship the statues. Since Islam came to Afghanistan until the present period the statues have not been damaged. The government regards the statues with serious respect and considers the position of their protection today to be the same as always. The government further considers the Bamiyan statues as an example of a potential major source of income for Afghanistan from international visitors.

Mullah Omar was even aware of the fears expressed by Buddhists worldwide, who had warned against damaging the statues. In that same decree, Mullah Omar said:

> Further, international Buddhist communities recently issued a warning that in case the Bamiyan statues are dam-

aged, then mosques will be damaged in their regions. The Muslims of the world are paying attention to this declaration. The Taliban government states that Bamiyan will not be destroyed but protected.

That decree wasn't a one-shot declaration.

In the August 10, 2000, issue of the *Gazetteer*, the official government record issued by the Taliban's Justice Ministry, the Taliban government was ordered "to take proper measures, with the help/cooperation of concerned institutions, for supporting preservation, maintenance and repair of cultural and/or historical monuments."

In August 2000, the Taliban even opened the crumbling National Museum in Kabul, heavily damaged and looted during the mujahedeen government's rule. It provided bin Laden with the opportunity he needed.

The Taliban who were closest to bin Laden, particularly Defense Minister Obeidullah and the deputy prime minister, Mullah Hassan, reacted with outrage to one of the museum's most prominent artifacts: a naked 2,000-year-old seated bodhisattva, made of baked clay, wearing only an earring, armband, and necklace.

Both men, whose ministries and personal wealth depended on bin Laden, publicly slapped the naked statue across the head and shoulders to show their disgust at its nakedness.

Bin Laden seized the moment: In the Taliban central council, he denounced the presence of statues anywhere in Afghanistan. Without mentioning them by name, it was clear he had his sights on the giant statues in Bamiyan.

Against the backdrop of new UN sanctions and increasingly belligerent international statements, the few remaining moderate Taliban voices were overwhelmed. Instead, bin Laden's hardliner rhetoric set the policy, and he campaigned vigorously for the destruction of the statues, knowing the symbolic value of the act. He knew it would cement the world's revulsion toward the Taliban.

No one listened to those seeking to preserve the statues, some of whom went to Mullah Hassan's home in Kabul during the peak of the debate to plead with him to save the statues.

The final decision was up to Mullah Omar, who sought bin Laden's direction. Bin Laden said destroy them. Taliban whom I met in early 2001 said the destruction order came from the foreigners but implementation was ordered by the Taliban central command.

In just sixteen months, Mullah Omar had made a complete about-face. It was the first time he had ever done that.

On February 26, 2001, an edict was issued in Mullah Omar's name. It read:

> Based on consulting of religious leaders of the Islamic Emirate of Afghanistan, the religious ulema judgments and supreme court of the Islamic Emirate of Afghanistan, all the statues located in different parts of the country must be broken. Because these statues have remained as a shrine of infidels and they are worshipping these statues and still the statues are being respected and probably it will be changed for shrines again, while God Almighty is the real shrine and the false shrines should be smashed.

The Taliban were reluctant to allow any outsiders near the statues before their destruction because they didn't want anyone to witness the truckloads of Arab fighters in the area. Nevertheless, in March 2001, the Taliban took a few journalists to Bamiyan. We were carefully controlled, and not allowed to wander far from the Taliban guards.

Amir Shah traveled with me on the first Ariana Airlines flight to Bamiyan since the 1980s Soviet invasion. We landed on a small plateau that stood opposite the giant statues.

We were piled into pickup trucks for the ride to where the statues had been. As we clattered along, two truckloads of fighters passed us. Amir Shah leaned toward me and whispered: "All of them are Arabs."

The destruction had been professional. The explosives that brought down the statues had left an outline of their grandeur. The mountain was undamaged. We weren't allowed to take any pieces from the site. The Taliban returned us quickly to the aircraft and sent us back to Kabul.

The destruction of the Buddha statues guaranteed that the rupture with the West would be permanent. Al Qaeda had to have been far along in its planning for the 9/11 attacks against the United States. Perhaps bin Laden was already thinking about the aftermath of those attacks. He knew he would need a sanctuary, a place where he could be sure he wouldn't be handed over, turned out of, the way Sudan had turned against him in 1996.

He needed the refuge that only a country that was irredeemably outside the international consensus could provide. Bin Laden helped create such a country with the destruction he brought to Afghanistan.

When he issued the edict ordering the statues destroyed, Mullah Omar became a symbol to Muslim extremists; he became the greatest of champions of Islam and his regime the purest of Islamic regimes.

How, then, could he ever hand over bin Laden, a great Islamic jihadist, a Muslim man who would achieve the most brutal mass murder on American soil in modern times? He could never betray such a man to infidels.

It was checkmate. Bin Laden had won.

CHAPTER SIX

The Last Days of the Taliban

On the morning of September 11, 2001, two stories were competing for the headlines in Kabul. The first story concerned the confused aftermath of an event that had taken place two days earlier in the Panjshir Valley. There, two Tunisians posing as journalists had blown up the iconic commander of the Northern Alliance, Ahmed Shah Massood. After that, the whole country was jumpy.

No one would confirm Massood's death. The Northern Alliance feared it would devastate a badly demoralized force already squeezed by the Taliban into a small mountainous corner of the country. One spokesman for the alliance said that Massood would be holding a press conference within days. Another one said he was being treated for his injuries just across the border in Tajikistan.

The truth was that he had died instantly. Mohammed Omar, one of Sayyaf's commanders who had been with Massood, later told me: "Massood died right away. It was a difficult time for us—day by day we were being isolated by the Taliban. Militarily we were not doing well. The morale of our troops had rested in Massood's hands."

The second story in the news that morning was unfolding in

Kabul, where attention focused on the ongoing month-long trial of eight Christian aid workers, including two young and very naive American women who had been accused by the Taliban of proselytizing—which was banned by the government.

Heather Mercer, who was just twenty-four, and Dayna Curry, who had celebrated her thirtieth birthday in Taliban custody, had tried to convert an Afghan employee at his home, putting not only themselves in danger but also the Afghans they were trying to convert.

It had been a bizarre couple of weeks. Each day, I went to the ratty nicotine-colored Supreme Court building. It had a Stalinist utilitarian look, a four-story, square cement building with no adornments. Inside, the halls were grimy and half the rooms had very little furniture, if any. I spent a lot of time in one waiting room that contained three desks, none of which had drawers that could be opened and one of which leaned slightly because one leg was somehow shorter than the rest. The chairs were all different and broken but still usable, providing you didn't move too much. A gray cabinet leaned against the wall for support, its legs missing, two of the four drawers hanging out and the other two nowhere in sight. There were small piles of dirt in the corners of the room.

The trial had dragged on interminably. It seemed that the Taliban were trying to make a point of the existence of their laws and legal system by showing how comprehensive they could be. The aid workers—the two Americans, four Germans, and two Australians—were charge-sheeted and given lawyers.

The Taliban even gave the eight their Bibles, but only the English versions. The Taliban kept their Pashtu- and Persian-language Bibles, afraid they might use them to try to convert their prison guards.

I had spent most of September 11, like the day before and the day before that, at the Supreme Court building, hoping to see the aid workers or to talk to the chief justice. When I returned to the office, it was just past 6 P.M., local time, or 9 A.M. in New York.

The satellite phone rang. The Associated Press foreign editor, Sally Jacobsen, was on the line. Her voice was calm. She called to tell me that a passenger plane had crashed into one of the World Trade Center towers. There was only confusion. No one knew whether it was an accident or a terrorist act, though once terrorism had been suggested, the name of Osama bin Laden became part of the conversation almost at once. He had become almost synonymous with terrorism: Virtually every attack against the United States in the preceding four years had been traced back to him and his al Qaeda organization. Bin Laden had reveled in the destruction, writing after the USS *Cole* was blown up off the coast of Yemen: "The pieces of the bodies of infidels were flying like dust particles. If you would have seen it with your own eyes, you would have been very pleased, and your heart would have been filled with joy."

While Sally was on the phone, the second plane slammed into the other World Trade Center tower. She hung up immediately. We knew what it meant.

In Afghanistan, it was surreal. There were no televisions. Afghans couldn't see those horrific images of the planes smashing into the World Trade Center towers, images that played over and over again and were burned into people's minds worldwide.

As the events unfolded, I felt as though I was on another planet. I, too, had no television, only a small radio. I fiddled with the dial, straining to hear through the wall of static, but could only find a Persian-language BBC channel. I couldn't see what was happening or understand what I was hearing.

After about thirty minutes, Amir Shah said a third plane had hit the Pentagon. By this time I didn't know what to think. And before I could digest that latest piece of news, Amir Shah began to shout so excitedly I could hardly understand him that there was a fourth aircraft missing, presumed hijacked by terrorists.

I couldn't imagine what the target might be, in fact I could hardly understand what was going on. We were in a vacuum. But I also knew we were about to be at the center of a violent and powerful storm. I pictured Afghanistan encased in a giant cocoon, cut off from the outside world yet tossed smack into the middle of the inferno that raged that day in the United States.

We knew only one place in Kabul where we could find a satellite television: the United Nations guest house, where the parents of the two American missionaries were staying.

Deborah Oddy, the mother of one of the accused missionaries, had only just arrived in Afghanistan from Lewiston, New York, earlier that day and had seen her daughter for the first time two hours before. She could hardly breathe as she watched the images, not sure what it meant. She was crying. By this time Heather's father, John Mercer, had already been in Afghanistan for weeks and had been haranguing the Taliban for visits with his daughter, trying to make sure she was safe, seeing her on occasion. Dayna's mother, Nancy Cassell, had also been in Kabul for weeks. Now none of them could imagine what lay ahead.

There, finally, I saw the horror inflicted by the four planes, hijacked, the controls taken over by madmen who had turned them into giant human-filled missiles and had driven them into the heart of America.

Could such a plot really have been masterminded from inside this backward country? The Taliban regime was not fired by the pan-Islamic dream that inspired some of the mujahedeen or bin Laden and his al Qaeda. They were backward tribesmen, most of whom had never even seen a computer. There was reportedly one computer in Kandahar, but it was controlled by Mullah Omar, who had no idea how to use it. He had never even turned it on. Mullah Omar was known to have come to Kabul only once, secretly, just for the purpose of inspiring his soldiers north of the city. It was widely said at the time that he hurried back to Kandahar, saying Kabul was too busy and too big.

Mullah Omar's idea of perfection was a world of simple truths that resembled Islam in the seventh century. The five years he ruled Afghanistan had been characterized by an attempt to go back in time. This regime banned recycled paper for fear Qurans had been destroyed and recycled into paper bags, banned women from wearing white socks because it was considered provocative, and relied mostly on radios to communicate.

But radical Islamists, some of whom had been in the country for decades, were not so backward. Bin Laden possessed sophisticated communications. I had talked to people who had seen them in northeastern Kunar Province, had heard him speak and heard foreign languages spoken back. One person reported having seen a North Korean with bin Laden teaching him about chemical weapons. He and Aymen al-Zawahri ran a global organization. They alone in Afghanistan had the money and the means to plot and execute the 9/11 attacks. Evidence that al Qaeda had become increasingly organized and militaristic in nature came from an eleven-volume Arabic-language *Encyclopedia of Jihad,* which was really a how-to manual on everything from storming secure sites to making and using explosives to conducting hijackings. A disgruntled Libyan had given it to me secretly several months earlier. He had been supposed to deliver it to an al Qaeda camp in eastern Afghanistan. The encyclopedias were being distributed to many of the camps run by the Arab militants. There were four dedication pages: one to bin Laden, one to Abdullah Azam, one to the Islamic leaders of Afghanistan, and one to Pakistan.

In May 2001, I had taken one volume to the CIA in Washington to obtain from them a background reading on what it might mean. At the time, the CIA didn't think it meant much.

Less than three hours after the attack, the Taliban's foreign minister, Wakil Ahmed Muttawakil, called a press conference at the war-ruined Intercontinental Hotel. The hulking five-story hotel, which perched on a hilltop overlooking the capital, was riddled with rocket damage from the years of mujahedeen rule. It was dark and dank. We gathered around a long table in a ground-floor meeting room.

Muttawakil, a stocky man with a round face and bushy black beard, looked genuinely distressed. He condemned the attack and denied any Taliban involvement. He said he didn't know the whereabouts of bin Laden: "I don't know where he is but I can tell you he isn't in this hotel."

We didn't know where Mullah Omar was, either. Later, a friend who had been in Kandahar on September 13 said the Taliban told him Mullah Omar had gone to Baghran, northwest of Kandahar.

The Taliban would not hand bin Laden over to the United States, Muttawakil said, but they would be willing to put him on trial in Afghanistan. The Taliban wanted proof of bin Laden's involvement in the attacks. Muttawakil wasn't anti-Western. He had tried to find a middle ground between the Taliban and the West. He had negotiated with the United Nations on several occasions, seeking assistance that would give strength to moderate voices and weaken the hard-liners, who eventually won out.

When Muttawakil left the hotel that night, the U.S. reaction to the attacks was still unclear. We had no way of knowing that it would be nearly a month before the United States would strike back. But Amir Shah succinctly expressed the fear of many Afghans: "Maybe America will set Afghanistan on fire."

Outside the UN guest house, the streets of Kabul were totally unchanged. On television, it was clear the world had turned on its axis; but in Kabul, it seemed as it always seemed, a little sluggish, dusty and dirty, the smell of open sewers nearby. Traffic was light; most people used bicycles. Except for the Taliban vehicles, the only other cars you usually saw on the streets were battered old yellow taxis. That night a few cars swerved down the potholed streets, their drivers heading home. Stores were closing. Electricity had been restored to most parts of Kabul, but not everyone had power. Open sewers ran along the sidewalks, and the few streetlights that worked were dingy and dim.

In Kabul, there were no celebrations over the news from New York. In some parts of the world, though, the dispossessed and angry celebrated; in the occupied West Bank, Palestinians danced around the flames of burning American flags, passed out sweets, a traditional show of joy. But that wasn't the way it was in Afghanistan.

Most Afghans had only the sketchiest of details, whatever they could pick up from the radio or from others in the street. They knew there had been an attack in the United States and many people were dead. Mostly, people in Kabul were mournful.

In a rundown drugstore that had only meager supplies of aspirin and old prescription medicine that had expired years earlier, the storekeeper, a man named Inayatullah, had been listening to the Pashtu- and Persian-language BBC broadcasts and the Taliban-run Radio Shariat, which quoted "foreign press reports" about the attacks. He said: "It's terrible. It makes me sad. No one can bear to see a country attacked. Everyone knows it is a crazy thing. It is a very bad action on humanity. Nobody, but nobody wants that criminal action."

One old man, walking slowly toward his home in the ruined Dasht-e-Barchi neighborhood, said he felt sadness for the people who died but that he didn't know where New York was and in fact didn't know what New York was. He had heard, though, of America and knew what it was like to be attacked. It was wrong.

When told that men had driven planes into office towers, he was utterly uncomprehending. An office building stretched a mile high? He thought we were crazy. The tallest building in Kabul was the eight-story Communications Ministry.

People were edgy that night. They had grown used to the idea that the United States wanted bin Laden and that the Taliban wouldn't give him up. They knew now that the United States would be angry, and even the poorest seemed to know that it would be their country that would suffer for the attacks. Most imagined the worst. People were so nervous that the engine noise of a low-flying aircraft that night sent everyone scurrying for cover. There were even a few surprised screams, even though the flight was just a routine Taliban transport coming into the airport.

I fell asleep that night sure the world would never be the same.

In the middle of the night, I was awakened by a phone call from the AP headquarters in New York because CNN was reporting that Kabul was under attack, possibly from the United States. Kabul was under curfew, so I couldn't go out to see what might be happening. It took me a few minutes to collect my thoughts. Suddenly, the house shuddered—and I did too. I was awake now.

New York was still on the phone. I was cautious and said it sounded like incoming rockets. There had been no jets and the concussions weren't powerful enough to be bombs.

From the balcony, I could see explosions from the neighborhood of the airport about two kilometers away. But there were no large fireballs. I could smell the acrid smoke lingering in the air. It was a confusing time. No one knew what to expect, whether to think the United States might retaliate immediately or wait.

Amir Shah got on the phone to the Northern Alliance. Throughout the Taliban rule we spoke to them, either in person or on the phone. Their spokesman denied the attack.

But by morning he had changed his mind and said Northern Alliance soldiers had used helicopter gunships to fire rockets into the airport. The Taliban wouldn't let us into the airport, but it seemed at least one passenger plane had been destroyed and several other aircraft, perhaps military, had sustained damage.

Abdul Jabbar, a day laborer who earned the equivalent of about $3 a month, lived near the airport. He said, "A helicopter came in and fired rockets at the airport. At first we were worrying that it was an attack by America, but then I thought it was stupid to worry—our life was so bad what difference does it make?"

Before even twenty-four hours had passed since the attacks in the United States, the United Nations sent in three emergency flights to evacuate its staff. Of the eighty UN staff in Afghanistan, only four remained in Kabul. But ordinary Afghans didn't think that the UN evacuation itself meant a retaliatory strike was imminent. Afghans were accustomed to the United Nations pulling out its international staff during particularly troubled times.

At the UN guest house, the parents of the two American missionaries were deeply distressed. John Mercer was angry. He had no intention of leaving his daughter behind in Afghanistan.

David Donahue, the consular officer from the U.S. Embassy in Pakistan, was in Afghanistan at the time and had been trying to convince John he had to leave.

The two American mothers sat silent, writing letters to their daughters, not sure when they would see them again.

They held out for one more day, but on September 13 the orders came from Washington to leave. Washington was very specific: It wanted David Donahue and the American parents he was shepherding out by 4 P.M. that day. David didn't know if that meant that air strikes were imminent. His orders had been terse, to the point.

John was like a caged bear. He paced the UN guest house. He drew David into a corner, argued with him, and pleaded to stay.

It wasn't clear when, or if, there would be a way back into Kabul by air after September 13. John wanted to know whether I would leave. I had decided to stay. He looked over at David, his eyes begging to stay. His jaw was clenched and I could almost hear his teeth grinding.

Several journalists also left. There were three flights that day, all of them evacuating international aid workers and their families. Once they had gone, it almost seemed too quiet, that eerie calm before a storm. All that remained in Kabul was a handful of International Red Cross workers.

The next day, September 14, was a Friday, the Muslim Sabbath. The mosques were full. The Taliban preachers in every mosque railed loud and hard against the United States. They warned of a possible attack and urged the faithful to find their strength in their faith. Most people just wanted to be left alone, and I couldn't find anyone who wanted to give Osama bin Laden refuge.

In Afghanistan, bin Laden, as well as Arab and foreign fighters, were called "guests." Mullah Omar, on more than one occasion, said it went against Afghan and Pashtun tradition to deny a guest sanctuary. Most Afghans, after 9/11, seemed to disagree.

"People are fed up with the guests. All our life has been burned by war and now because of them we will only get more," Mohammed Haroon, who owned a confectionery store in Kabul, said that day, returning from the mosque.

A Taliban echoed him: "These Arabs are not on the side of our nation. They are here for their own aim. I am afraid for our future."

No obvious preparations were made in Kabul for an attack. The Taliban ministries, such as they were, continued to function. The only evidence of anticipation came from the Arabs. In the first days after the attack on the United States, several trucks packed with household goods and Arab families rattled past. I could see women and children. I heard later that they had been evacuated to Logar Province, where a small colony of Arabs lived.

By September 14, all Westerners had been ordered out of Afghanistan. The order, it would seem, was bin Laden's doing. Afghans didn't see Westerners as spies, not even the Taliban. But the Arab fighters saw a spy in every Westerner. Al Jazeera television reporters stayed, as did Islamic charity organizations. But everyone else, including the Red Cross, had to go.

Pakistan was closing its border with Afghanistan. I left Kabul that day.

※

Mullah Omar was given a choice: Hand over bin Laden and his al Qaeda network or be attacked. Pakistan, which until then had supported the Taliban wholeheartedly, was called upon by Washington to open talks with Mullah Omar to persuade him to hand over bin Laden.

General Mahmood Ahmed, the chief of the ISI, Pakistan's intelligence service, led a group that also included some Muslim clerics. They went to Kandahar, supposedly to convince Mullah Omar to do the right thing.

The general was a religious zealot very much like Mullah Omar. He had been central to the military takeover of Pakistan in 1999 by General Pervez Musharraf. A hawk with pan-Islamic visions, he had been a staunch supporter of jihadis both from Pakistan and elsewhere. This was the man Musharraf sent to negotiate with Mullah Omar.

People present at the meeting and within the ISI revealed that Ahmed had a message for Mullah Omar quite different from the one that Washington had pressed his government to convey. He took the slow-talking Taliban leader aside and urged him to resist the United States. He told Mullah Omar not to give up bin Laden.

Ahmed traveled several times to Kandahar, and on each visit he gave Mullah Omar information about the likely next move by the United States. By then Ahmed knew there weren't going to be a lot of U.S. soldiers on the ground. He warned Mullah Omar that the United States would be relying heavily on aerial bombardment and on the Northern Alliance.

Two weeks after the attacks on the United States, the immediate fear of a devastating retaliatory strike had passed and some within the Taliban had begun to think they could survive a U.S. assault. After all, one Taliban told me, they had survived the U.S. missile attack in 1998. Could this time be worse? He had no idea of the firepower the United States could bring to bear.

They had no concept of the magnitude of the events that had occurred in the United States. Neither Osama bin Laden nor Pakistan's ISI chief explained to Mullah Omar the extent of the devastation that would be linked to his name and his movement.

Instead, bin Laden talked to Mullah Omar about the Hadiths (the sayings of the prophet). Bin Laden debated the Quran at length with Mullah Omar and brought up the words of Islam's prophet that exhort the faithful to keep faith with fellow Muslims, to protect them against aggressors.

From Ahmed, Mullah Omar got military pointers. Mullah Omar didn't know what targets the United States would hit. The

Afghan military didn't have any real command-and-control system; their antiaircraft defenses were guns on hilltops. Mullah Omar also didn't know what weaponry would be available to the United States. He didn't know anything of the 'daisy cutters' that could supposedly reach deep into caves and destroy everything inside. He couldn't even conceive of a sophisticated fighter jet. Mullah Omar's only experience with U.S. firepower had been the Tomahawk cruise missiles attack of 1998, which had done very little damage.

General Mahmood Ahmed also met other Taliban allies, such as Jalaluddin Haqqani, a former mujahedeen who had been to the White House during the 1980s Soviet invasion of Afghanistan, who was allied with the Taliban. He was also close to bin Laden and al Qaeda, whose training camps were in eastern Afghanistan's Khost region, controlled by Haqqani.

Had he wanted to, Haqqani could have handed the United States the entire al Qaeda network. Pakistan's ISI chief warned him against it. Just days before the strike on Afghanistan, Haqqani made a secret visit to Pakistan. He met Ahmed in Rawalpindi, where the military is headquartered, just a few miles from the Pakistani capital. Ahmed told him to hold out, that he had friends across the border.

When the strike finally came on October 7, 2001, only a few thousand U.S. soldiers were amassed to launch a ground offensive against the Taliban. Even among the Americans at the U.S. Embassy in Pakistan, there was surprise at the small number of American ground forces deployed.

A former defense official with decades of experience in the region said: "Those of us in the embassy were puzzled in the run-up to Operation Enduring Freedom as to why so few troops were being put on the ground to defeat the Taliban. In hindsight, though, the administration's apparent plan for a follow-on campaign in Iraq explains the small number of boots put on the ground in Afghanistan." Instead, the United States and its coalition partners relied on the Northern Alliance.

It was an astonishing act of delegation. The Northern Alliance had close links with the Arab militants, with such men as Aymen al-Zawahri, who had been in Afghanistan since 1985. The small number of U.S. forces that were put on the ground in Afghanistan had to rely on these Northern Alliance soldiers for their intelligence, which might explain why they were unable to find either bin Laden or Aymen al-Zawahri.

Both bin Laden and al-Zawahri had been members of Sayyaf's mujahedeen group and in close alliance with Sayyaf, who was the Northern Alliance's deputy prime minister.

The Northern Alliance soldiers were also poor fighters. The Taliban had driven them into a small corner of the country. After the death of Ahmed Shah Massood, they became demoralized and leaderless—hardly perfect allies.

It was American and British bombing that won the war, not the Northern Alliance soldiers. Early on in the offensive, the Northern Alliance soldiers did make a push for the northern city of Mazar-e-Sharif ahead of any heavy bombing. They were easily beaten back by the Taliban. When the city finally fell, it was after massive bombing of Taliban positions and front lines, which drove the Taliban either out of the city or to surrender.

Some of the hard-line clerics in Pakistani religious schools closed them down and sent their students to Afghanistan to fight for the Taliban. They fired them up with the spirit of jihad and sent them across the border, sometimes by the hundreds. The students, some as young as sixteen, didn't know what they were getting into.

I met one young jihadi sent from Pakistan by his teacher, who stayed behind in the safety of his school. The young boy was terrified. He was barely sixteen years old, wearing a uniform that looked three sizes too big. The shirt hung off his small frame; his hands were lost inside the sleeves. The Northern Alliance had captured him. He was trembling, terrified of what might happen to him.

His teacher had told him he would fight infidels. Although he had been on the front lines north of Kabul, he had not seen any infidels, he said.

There was only bombing, every day, all day. The noise, the concussions, the death had frightened him. He fled. He covered his face with dirt and grabbed some vegetables, pretending to be an Afghan, hoping to escape.

Amir Shah pleaded with his captors to send him home. "He's just a boy. He can't hurt anyone. You have children, let him go home." When we left, he was still in the custody of the Northern Alliance.

One Pakistani cleric, Sufi Mohammed, sent several thousand boys from his madrassa to Afghanistan. Most of them died when U.S. bombers pounded a school in northern Afghanistan. Those who survived were taken prisoner.

In those first weeks of the war, the Taliban refused to allow any foreigners into the territory they held, which was most of the country. Al Jazeera and our Afghan colleagues were alone in Kabul.

The Taliban didn't allow photography or videotaping. But Amir Shah was brilliant, brave, and uncanny, and he managed to do both. He had a handheld video camera, and one day when he was filming, a couple of Taliban soldiers surprised him. He thought fast. With one quick motion he put the camera to his ear, pretended it was a radio, and said: "Brothers, it's the BBC." They had seen so few cameras that they believed him.

During the first weeks of the war, Amir Shah would call each night in Islamabad, his voice a rapid whisper. Only I would speak to him because he had to be fast, using as few words as possible to get the information out.

Each day we pleaded with the Taliban to let me return, and each day the answer was the same. I wasn't alone trying to get into the Taliban's Afghanistan. There were hundreds of reporters camped out in Pakistan, going every day to the Afghan Embassy pleading for permission to go to Afghanistan.

Eventually, because of Amir Shah's persistence, we succeeded where everyone else had failed. No other foreign reporter was allowed in. Amir Shah got permission from the information minister, Qadratullah Jamal, who convinced Kandahar to make an exception.

Getting into Afghanistan was important to me not just to cover the Taliban but to report on ordinary Afghans, caught again in another conflict not of their making.

I was allowed to bring our photographer, Dimitri Messinis, a big strapping Greek with a sensitive and beautiful photographer's eye and an expansive and generous heart that embraced the Afghans he met.

My first night back in Afghanistan was October 24, 2001. At 9 P.M., suddenly everything went dark. Every night at the same time, the Taliban shut off the electricity, plunging the city into blackness, apparently unaware that pilots in those fighter jets flying overhead didn't need lights to see their targets.

Jets roared distantly overhead until one came closer. We waited and watched from the upstairs windows of our darkened house. The sound of the jet engine changed, growing louder as the jet dropped altitude, preparing for a bombing run.

"Listen," Amir Shah whispered. A powerful concussion shook the house, rattling the windows in their frames. It was scary. But more frightening was Amir Shah's soft whisper: "Oh my God. Oh my God."

The second night was worse.

Powerful explosions, one after another, pounded the ground throughout the night. An ammunition depot was hit nearby. The detonations were deafening. Heavy artillery exploded, rockets roared. All the Taliban could do was take aim at the fighter jets with their antiquated antiaircraft guns. The pounding of the bombs was relentless.

Sher Aga, our elderly gray-bearded guard, crouched against a far wall, hugged his knees to his chest, his frail hands trembling.

We slept upstairs the first night. It was pitch black outside, and everyone in our neighborhood was inside, quiet. No one had a telephone except us. I worried it would ring. We were directly across the street from the Taliban's vice and virtue minister.

The Wazir Akbar Khan neighborhood of Kabul where we were situated was one of the better areas of the city and home to most of the Taliban leaders as well as many Arabs, Chechens, and Uzbeks.

A telephone ringing in the one house in Kabul in which a Westerner was living could quite easily arouse suspicions among our Arab neighbors, who already thought any Westerner in Kabul could only be there to guide the U.S. and British fighter jets overhead.

Those first days were filled with uncertainty. It wasn't clear where the Arab fighters had dispersed to. Were they on the front line north of Kabul? Had they returned to the city? Would they know I was in Kabul? What would they do if they found out? Amir Shah was nervous: For three weeks he would have the only Western journalist in Kabul to worry about, as well as himself and his family.

The bombing generally stopped during the day. You could hear the aircraft heading further north, pounding front lines away from Kabul. It was then possible to move around, find out what had happened the night before. For most of that last week in October 2001, the bombing in and around the city was intense. The allied planes were trying to take out the telecommunications towers, which actually hadn't been working in years, and were also targeting the antiaircraft positions dotted around the hills that ringed Kabul.

I had been back in Kabul only a couple of days when we went to see what the bombing had achieved in the shadow of the hills. The neighborhood, poor already, was a dusty brown color; the homes were shabby brick buildings. Bombs had flattened three houses the night before.

Inside on a dirty table in one building were the bodies of three children; the oldest cannot have been more than five or six years old. A man, weeping silently, was rubbing them, cleaning them.

Their tiny bodies were covered, it seemed, in a layer of fine dust. I looked at the face of the little girl. Her hair was cropped and matted with dust.

Amir Shah took pictures; his hands were shaking.

The crying outside was loud and horribly wracked with pain. A woman collapsed near me. I was afraid they would be angry, that they would take their anger out on me. But instead, one woman just clung to my hand and held it tightly to her face. She wouldn't let me go. She just clutched my hand. I could feel myself fighting back the tears.

Nine people, all from the same family, were dead. The only survivor was a thirteen-year-old boy. He had been taken to the Wazir Akbar Khan Hospital. I found him in a room at the end of a narrow dark corridor. Doctors clustered around him.

He was in shock, perhaps. He lay trembling beneath several woolen blankets blackened with dirt. He didn't know what had happened. He remembered the bombing. He said he had been so afraid. Again and again the bombs fell. But he didn't remember his home being hit or his family being killed.

His mother's sister was holding his hand, gently. It looked as if it had been shredded by glass. One side of his body was badly burned.

I looked at his face. It was swollen, and a bloodied white bandage covered his one eye. Beneath the bandage the socket was empty.

His aunt was too afraid to tell him what had happened, afraid he would not recover from his wounds. So she lied. She told him he had been sleepwalking and had fallen down a well.

Later that same day, back in the office, I looked over at Amir Shah, who was staring at the pictures of the dead children on his computer screen. His head seemed heavy. He looked at me and said, "I get so scared because I see *my* children lying there and I think what if I come home in the morning and my house is gone, my children are dead." His voice just trailed off.

I couldn't offer any comfort or reassurance. Amir Shah stayed the nights at the office but each morning hurried to his home in the Taimani neighborhood of Kabul, far from the surrounding hills and from any military installation, to check on his family.

During those weeks in Kabul, official life attempted to function normally. Although the Health Ministry building had no doors, the health minister was in his office. The Telecommunications Ministry had no electricity, but people paid their bills. Bureaucrats who had been working for the government for decades were at their desks.

It was only at night the fear really set in—when 9 P.M. rolled around, the lights went out, and the bombing began again. The targets inside Kabul were places like the ammunition depots or the army headquarters, both in the middle of Kabul.

One day we went to the Central Bank. I decided to use the bank to change some money rather than go to the money changers squatting out on the street.

I stepped into the bank's main foyer. It was empty except for a broken clock hanging alone on a pillar. Stairs led up to small offices nearby. I took the steps gingerly because the carpet had come loose, probably ten years earlier, and with every step the whole thing felt as though it would slide away beneath my feet and carry me with it.

I finally found the room I needed. It was cavernous and cold. Inside, fewer than a dozen men were at their desks. They didn't seem busy. Everyone stopped when I walked in. They hadn't seen a Westerner in nearly two months. What did it mean? All they wanted to know was whether my being there meant the war would soon be over.

Outside on the rocket-ruined streets, black trucks rumbled throughout the capital carrying hulking antiaircraft guns sheathed in black tarpaulins. In the evening the tarps were taken off when bombardment by U.S. jets resumed—and Taliban antiaircraft guns once again came to life.

Fuel trucks, another target of the bombers, were hidden beneath trees in a park in the middle of Kabul.

At night, the only traffic on the street belonged to the Taliban militia. Ordinary Afghans were under curfew. Most people cowered in their homes, listening to the rattle of the antiaircraft fire that usually followed the concussive roar of bomb strikes. Parents tried to comfort screaming, frightened children.

No food was getting into Kabul. The markets still had vegetables and fruit, but they were expensive. Most of the international aid agencies had left Kabul, but the Taliban had allowed the Arab and Islamic charities to stay.

One day we came across the International Relief Agency, a Canadian-based Islamic charity. They were distributing bags of flour in front of a mosque. The scene was chaotic. People were pushing and shoving trying to get to the bags of flour. The charity had only 220 sacks to give out, and there must have been hundreds in need. People were desperate.

Fazl Karim, a nurse at Wazir Akbar Khan Hospital, hardly had the energy to fight for one bag of flour. His eyes were heavy and bloodshot. His hands seemed too weak to hold the flour. He mourned: "I don't care if I die, because we have nothing. No power, no food, nothing. Only the poorest are living here."

He said that every day at the hospital was a relentless struggle. The Wazir Akbar Khan Hospital was in a particularly dangerous area, not far from the airport or the military garrison and near a hill from which the Taliban fired antiaircraft guns.

It was a terrifying place to be during the bombing. The facility was four stories tall, but every night all the patients were hustled down the wide wooden stairs to the basement. Dirty-burning kerosene lamps provided the only light. There was no diesel for the generator. Karim said an appendectomy had to be postponed for lack of electricity.

A ten-year-old boy with shrapnel wounds had been brought in, his name logged carefully and neatly by the nurse. But the hospital had no anesthetic for operations, so the doctors could not treat him. Instead, they just logged his name to recognize his death.

❧

The Taliban's information minister, Qadratullah Jamal, had warned me that not everyone welcomed my presence. He was referring mainly to the Arab militants, but he also thought that residents terrorized by nightly bombing raids might attack the only Westerner in town. As I listened to him, my eyes fixed on his bushy black beard and turban, I was struck by the irony of the fact that the only Western reporter that the Taliban, the most misogynistic of regimes, had allowed back into Kabul was a woman.

I remembered a comment from a Taliban visa officer at the end of a particularly heated discussion. He stopped talking, looked at me, and said: "We have a name for a person like you—a man."

It was hardly a surprise when, in the first few days of my arrival in Kabul, military intelligence stormed our office, grabbed our equipment, and hauled us off to a compound, on the southeastern edge of Kabul, referred to as Intelligence No. 2. An intelligence officer thought I was in Kabul secretly, without Taliban approval.

His tone was belligerent. He was ready to throw me in jail or out of Kabul. But Amir Shah had all the permission slips he needed. The signature on them was that of the Taliban's prime minister, Mullah Hassan, the second most powerful authority in the movement after Mullah Omar.

It was good enough for the commander, who relaxed noticeably and offered us green tea. He pulled out a pistol and waved it in my face, not in a menacing way, but to show me what he would use to face down the U.S. soldiers. He bragged, "I need this for when the American commandos come."

This office was large and dirty. The brown carpet on the floor was stained and turned up at the edges. The coffee table was caked in dust. The commander said he and his staff spent most of their time in the basement because of the bombing.

The windows were open as a precaution: Should a bomb drop nearby, the glass wouldn't blow in. I didn't feel particularly comforted. I could hear fighter jets overhead. It was mid-afternoon. I hoped they wouldn't bomb out of schedule. As much as I wanted to return to the safety of the house I was living in, the commander wanted to talk. We sat there for another thirty minutes sipping sugary green tea in greasy old cups that appeared not to have been washed since the war began. The interview at least gave me the chance to ask again after the two Christian aid workers, who now found themselves in the truly hellish position of being in a remote foreign jail in a city that was being bombed by their countrymen.

Eventually, I found out where they were being held. One of their guards was an old man, spindly and gray, who talked to me every morning about what they had had to eat. The women were held together in one compound, and the male Christian aid detainees were nearby.

The guard said his name was Hajji Sahab, although I don't think he had ever performed the Muslim pilgrimage of Hajj. He was happy to give me the daily news of their condition. I had tried to get permission to see them, but the Taliban refused.

Hajji Sahab was happy to talk to anyone, not minding that I was a Westerner, even though it was the West that was bombing his country.

He reflected: "We're poor, we have nothing. What can they take from us? Nothing." The bombs terrified him, though. At night he was usually on guard, and sometimes he said he would hear the girls singing, sometimes it seemed when the bombing was the heaviest, their voices were the loudest.

I was keeping in touch by satellite telephone with the parents of the two American women, and each day I would let them know their children were safe. John wanted a mass of detailed information about the location of his daughter's compound. I understood he was asking because he wanted to let the U.S. military know exactly where Heather was.

೫⊰೪

By November 12, 2001, it seemed the Taliban could not hang on much longer. They had already lost Mazar-e-Sharif and much of northern Afghanistan. A battle continued to rage in northern Kunduz Province, and southern Kandahar was still in Taliban hands. But it looked as if Kabul would fall.

Amir Shah talked by telephone to Abdul Rasul Sayyaf of the Northern Alliance. The United States had stated publicly that the Northern Alliance would keep its private militias out of Kabul once the capital fell to prevent chaos, thieving, and killing. Amir Shah asked Sayyaf whether his militia would observe the restriction. Sayyaf laughed and said, "Brother, of course we will be in Kabul. No one will keep us out." The mobs were coming back.

That same day was the closest I came to being blown up by the bombing. I was upstairs in the AP house on the satellite phone talking to my husband in Pakistan. We talked daily, sometimes twice and three times a day. It was my comfort, but I had sometimes wondered whether the United States might pick up the signal from the satellite phone and wrongly think it belonged to the Taliban.

We hadn't been talking for more than a few minutes when a sudden and powerful explosion threw me across the room. The glass windows rushed in. I found myself on the floor at the other end of the room, my back to the window. My foot was bleeding. I had lost my glasses. As I staggered down the stairs, I met Amir Shah, climbing the steps two at a time to see how I was. The front door had been blown off its frame and all the windows were shattered.

We ran out of the house. It was hard to see exactly where the bomb had landed. It was nearby: The air was thick with smoke and dust. Through the haze, I saw a woman in her pale blue burqa running down the street toward us. She was screaming, and behind her were her three children, all crying. They looked completely terrified. Perhaps it was the circumstances, but I couldn't remember seeing such fear before. We hustled them into the basement of the house.

By nightfall, it was clear that the war had begun a new phase. Targeted rocketing broke out, which meant that our neighborhood, full of the Arabs, Chechens, Uzbeks, and Pakistani jihadis, would be extremely dangerous.

We decided to leave the house and the neighborhood, but first we drove, in reverse, a half a block to a house where, two days earlier, the Taliban had let the BBC bring four people into Kabul. They crammed into our small yellow taxi, and together we decided to try to get to the Intercontinental Hotel, just fifteen minutes away.

We could hear the B-52s overhead. The devastation of war was encroaching: I looked to the side and saw a destroyed pickup truck. Four Arabs had been killed when a missile slammed into it. We didn't stop until we came to a Taliban roadblock, which was a scene of utter chaos.

Four pickup trucks blocked our way, all packed with Taliban soldiers armed with rifles and rocket launchers and talking nervously, shouting into static-filled two-way radios, yelling into our car, screaming at us in Pashtu.

They wanted to know what foreigners were doing in Kabul. Their voices were hysterical, full of accusations about America, about the planes and the bombing. It wasn't good.

Amir Shah spoke softly. He cajoled them, showed them our documents. It seemed to take forever. We could hear the jets overhead. They were bombing, and we were right in the middle of a perfect target, dozens of Taliban in pickup trucks.

Just as I was trying to decide whether to get out of the car and hug the nearest wall, a motorcycle roared passed. It was carrying two Arab fighters.

Eventually, they let us go. We had one more checkpoint to get through and then we would be at the Intercontinental Hotel.

At one of the checkpoints, a young Taliban had been ordered to accompany us. He was nervous. He clung to a small handheld two-way radio into which he kept chattering. He was still receiving orders from someone, but it was obviously just a matter of time before communications and the Taliban command broke down.

News came that the Al Jazeera office had taken a direct hit, but no one was hurt. The bombing that night was pretty precise, and there was no doubt in anyone's mind that Al Jazeera had been deliberately targeted. Throughout the bombing, Al Jazeera had been the only television station broadcasting. The correspondent had interviewed bin Laden.

At 9 P.M., like clockwork, the power went off and the Intercontinental Hotel, still riddled with gaping holes from the mujahedeen years, was thrown into darkness like the rest of the city.

I went to my room, which was right next to Amir Shah. I had a candle and lots of matches. I lay in bed in the dark, listening to and feeling the crashing concussions of the bombs, followed by the antiaircraft fire.

Every now and again, I would light my candle just to reassure myself that I knew exactly where it was.

What I didn't know was that the Taliban leadership had already planned their departure. They had met at 6 P.M. that night at the home of Mullah Hassan, the prime minister.

While U.S. and British bombs pummeled their foot soldiers on the front lines north of Kabul, the Taliban leadership discussed strategy. They would decide how to leave, where to go, where to set up the new front line, where to regroup.

The bombing in Kabul that night had been intense. Homes of Taliban leaders were targeted, but they were empty. Bombs flattened the police chief's house and the home of Mullah Dadullah, a powerful Taliban commander who has still eluded capture.

Several of the others who were at that farewell meeting at Mullah Hassan's have also evaded capture. Qadratullah Jamal, the culture and information minister was there and is still free, some say in Pakistan. Mullah Mohammed Abbas, the health minister, escaped as well, some say by pretending to be a nomad and moving through the countryside undetected. His deputy minister, Sher Mohammed Stanikzai, a small man with a wispy black beard who spoke perfect English, was there and escaped. Interior Minister Abdul Razzak was there and also escaped, some say to Chaman on the border with Pakistan.

The Taliban leaders gathered at Mullah Hassan's agreed to meet sometime after 10 P.M. at a small place called Durrani, about fifty miles south of Kabul, with the intention of establishing two new front lines, one at Durrani and another southeast of Kabul at Sang-e-Nowishta. In fact, they failed: The bombing drove them further south toward Kandahar.

፠

Amir Shah and I stepped out on the hotel balcony at about 6 A.M. on November 13. The sun was just peeking over the foothills of the Hindu Kush Mountains. We left the hotel and went back to the Taliban checkpoint that had been so frightening the night before. It was deserted. We kept driving. A few scattered bodies across from the UN guest house appeared to be Arab fighters. Four more burned bodies lay slumped inside a charred pickup.

The blistering bombing campaign administered by the United States and Britain had driven the Taliban out of Kabul and had allowed the Northern Alliance to walk in. The alliance forces brought with them their militias, who took over the homes abandoned by the Taliban, rampaged through some neighborhoods, and stole from residents. People were frightened. They mostly stayed indoors.

My first stop was at the compound where the Christian aid workers had been held. Hajji Sahab, the elderly guard, was still there, but the aid workers were gone. Other guards at the compound spoke feverishly, their words tumbling out as they recalled the events of the previous nights. It had been chaos after the Taliban left.

The Taliban had taken the aid workers when they fled. As it turned out, the Taliban probably saved their lives, or certainly saved the two young American girls from attacks by Northern Alliance militiamen.

Several Northern Alliance men had come looking for the American women. One guard recalled the conversation: "Three different times, the militiamen came, and one said: 'Where is the tall, pretty one. Where is she?' And another one said: 'I know there were two young pretty girls. Where are they?' I don't know what they would have done if they had been here. We told them they were gone. The Taliban took them."

I called Heather's father, John. I tried to reassure him that as bizarre as it sounded, his daughter was probably lucky the Taliban had taken them out of Kabul that night. I gave him details, told him the color of the car they had been seen leaving in and the direction in which it was headed. I found out later that the U.S. military used that information, and an American security guard at the U.S. Embassy told me that information had saved their lives. Fighter pilots had spotted the convoy and had been going to attack until they were called off. It also gave the U.S. Special Forces, who eventually rescued the aid workers, something to look for.

But that would happen later.

On November 13, as we picked our way back to our shattered office, the only thing we knew for sure was that the battle for Kabul was over. The Taliban were gone.

Wanted terrorist and former U.S. ally Gulbuddin Hekmatyar during the 1980s Soviet war, when he was heavily financed by the United States along with Jalaluddin Haqqani, a wanted man today in hiding somewhere in the border regions of Pakistan.

Hekmatyar walks past a guard of honor in Pakistan after being named interim prime minister of Afghanistan in 1992.

Hekmatyar is sworn in as prime minister in 1996 by Burhanuddin Rabbani. Looking on is Abdul Rasul Sayyaf, a current U.S. ally. Hekmatyar was sworn in after four years of brutal factional fighting that killed 50,000 Afghans. He was fighting both Rabbani and Sayyaf.

At the Torkham border post in Afghanistan, author Kathy Gannon argues with Taliban border sergeant Mullah Hanifi, as AP correspondent Riaz Khan looks on. Gannon was at the border post en route to Kabul in October 2001—becoming the only western journalist allowed back into Afghanistan by the Taliban before their eventual retreat from Kabul on Nov. 13, 2001.

In an attempt to enlist the help of Afghans, the United States dropped tens of thousands of leaflets throughout the countryside depicting Taliban soldiers beating women. The accompanying words both in Farsi and Pashtu, Afghanistan's two national languages, seek help in finding Taliban remnants, saying the Taliban were harsh and cruel.

The tortured and bloated body of Afghanistan's former communist president, Najibullah, hangs in the Kabul town square—put there by Taliban soldiers when they took control of Kabul in September 1996. One of the first acts of the Taliban, some of whom had lost several relatives in the 1980s anti-communist war, was to take revenge and hang Najibullah and his brother.

Hundreds of turbaned Taliban, bristling with weapons, roared through the parade grounds in Kabul in 2001 while celebrating Afghanistan's independence. The celebration came less than two months before the Sept. 11, 2001 attacks against the United States.

Taliban escort Christian missionaries, including two American women, back to their cells after a court appearance in Kabul. The missionaries were charged with proselytizing—a crime in the Taliban's Afghanistan. When the Taliban fled Kabul on Nov. 13, 2001, they took the missionaries with them, probably saving their lives, or at least those of the two American girls, who were sought out by marauding Northern Alliance men looking for the "pretty" American girls.

At the border between Afghanistan and Pakistan, Amir Shah, left, sets up a satellite telephone to allow Mullah Hanifi, the Taliban sergeant, to call Kabul and get the go-ahead to let us into the capital, where we became the only western journalists to be allowed into Afghanistan after Sept. 11, 2001 and before the religious militia fled the city on Nov. 13, 2001. Dimitri Messinis, an AP photographer, is next to Hanifi and beside him, hidden beneath the black and white scarf, is the author.

Mullah Mohammed Khaksar, former Taliban intelligence chief and one of the founders of the religious movement, shows one half of a five rupee note he received after meeting U.S. CIA officials in neighboring Pakistan nearly two years before the Sept. 11, 2001 attacks, offering to get Osama bin Laden and defeat the Taliban. The CIA refused. Khaksar stayed behind when the Taliban fled.

The Taliban destroyed two giant statues of Buddha, hewn from a sandstone mountain in the third and fifth centuries. The Buddhas were destroyed after Osama bin Laden told Taliban leader Mullah Omar that they were blasphemous to Islam and should be removed. The world was outraged.

Abdul Rasul Sayyaf, a current U.S. ally, was among the mujahedeen leaders in power in Afghanistan—the ones who welcomed Osama bin Laden to Afghanistan in 1996 from Sudan, where he had been forced to leave under U.S. pressure. Sayyaf, whose men carried out brutal atrocities during the mujahedeen's rule, was a close ally of Ahmed Shah Massood, on the right in this photograph, whose men also carried out brutal acts. Massood was killed on Sept. 9, 2001 by Tunisian suicide bombers.

CHAPTER SEVEN

After the Taliban

Surmad wasn't much to look at. It was a small, dusty town with little to distinguish it. Its homes were difficult to see, hidden behind high walls. Some were outfitted with turrets. But for the fact that the guards carried rifles instead of bows and arrows, it might well have been the Middle Ages. The centuries seemed to have slipped past unnoticed in Surmad. Men wore the traditional dress and turbans of their ancestors. Women were neither seen nor heard. There was only one main street and it had never seen pavement. The buildings were a strange mix of cement and mud baked in the blistering sun.

Rarely was anything easy in Afghanistan. But on this day in December 2001, getting into Surmad seemed a particular torture.

It was a painful thirty-five-minute car journey from eastern Afghanistan's city of Gardez, where the paved road gave out. In its place, the road resembled a dried riverbed and the taxi grumbled as we bumped and rattled our way toward Surmad.

As I choked back the dust, I wondered whether the trip was worth the effort. I had never been to Surmad, but its history was intriguing.

Surmad had been a Taliban stronghold to rival Kandahar. It had given up more sons to the Taliban than any other town in Afghanistan, other than perhaps Kandahar. It had produced several Taliban ministers. They, too, were an odd bunch. The information minister, Qadratullah Jamal, was a confounding mix: One day he would help journalists who were harassed by the likes of the murderous intelligence minister, and the next day he would cheer on the destruction of the giant Buddha statues. Then there was the intimidating agriculture minister, Mansour Latif, a deeply conservative man who occasionally made Mullah Omar seem tolerant; and his nephew Saif-ur Rahman, who had been disfigured by shrapnel. His left hand was mangled and useless, his face pockmarked with scars. Several months after my visit, Saif-ur Rahman would lead Arab and Chechen fighters in the snow-dusted mountains behind Surmad against U.S. soldiers in Operation Anaconda, the Pentagon's biggest ground offensive of the Afghan war.

But none would be in Surmad for my first visit, just two weeks since the Taliban's countrywide routing. They had hung on in Kandahar until December 7, finally negotiating their departure with Hamid Karzai in a mountain hideout in Uruzgan Province and ending a bloody standoff, sustained more by their Arab militant allies than by the Taliban. The survivors, including Mullah Omar, had faded away into the mountains.

At first glance, Surmad appeared as a small Taliban enclave that had survived the coalition's onslaught. A steel barricade blocked the road. On either side, badly dented spent shells had been pounded into the crusty earth. It was a fierce-looking band of five men, their heads swathed in black turbans, aiming their rifles in our direction that stopped our car. Silently, they motioned us to pull over.

Finally, one of the five leaned into the car. He wasn't smiling, and Amir Shah did the first thing Afghans always do when they meet. He offered his hand.

The threatening poses disappeared, replaced by curiosity about who the foreigner was. The turbaned guard whose head was poking in at us was Abdul Jan, a lean, lanky man of barely twenty-five years. He and Amir Shah exchanged a few words in his native Pashtu before he slipped his hand inside his vest pocket and pulled out a cassette tape. "Play it," he ordered. Music soon wheezed from the car's cheap speakers. The singer's voice was painfully screechy, and the accompaniment was a pounding drum and a whiny instrument but our bearded guards enjoyed it.

We were listening to the Afghan equivalent of Janis Joplin. Abdul Jan was a happy man: "See, the Taliban are gone."

Had the Taliban still been around, Abdul Jan would have been badly beaten, his cassette ripped from the car stereo and destroyed.

We didn't get to see too much of Surmad that trip. Abdul Jan, our escort, took long, quick strides through narrow streets. I studied his face, already lined and worn looking. His beard was scrawny and sprinkled with dust. His turban was disheveled, unraveling at one end, and his clothes were grimy and worn. I looked down at his dirt-blackened feet and saw they were tucked inside a pair of purple plastic sandals.

We stopped outside a high wall that surrounded a compound of modest houses. There was a stillness in the air; the sky was clear and the sun bright overhead. Abdul Jan didn't seem anxious, but he had been careful not to tell us where we were going.

Men with Kalashnikovs lazed outside, and inside in a large carpeted room sat several big burly men, their combined bulk straining an ornate couch that hugged one wall.

We were introduced to Mohammed Faruqi, the leanest of the men, with a long black beard and a holster that peeked out from beneath his shawl. He was the town's police chief. I recognized him, though I didn't initially say so. He had been in Kabul a lot during the Taliban regime, but I couldn't place him. Had he been one of the ministers or a bureaucrat, or had he perhaps worked in the Interior Ministry? After struggling to place him, finally I asked him outright. He recoiled, his voice suddenly tense and angry: "We had nothing to do with the Taliban. They were the government, that's all; we had business sometimes in Kabul. But we were not a part of the Taliban."

His eyes were a deep mesmerizing brown. They looked larger because of the black kohl, something akin to eyeliner, that Afghan men often wear.

His voice was strong and firm. He wanted me to understand. He was happy the Taliban were gone. His reasons were pretty basic. It wasn't about the Taliban's treatment of women. There he thought they were right. Women should be in the home and should be covered, and security under the Taliban had been good. But it was the Taliban's restrictions on the men that bothered him and the others on the couch. They had resented the Taliban's encroachment on their personal lives and that it was always Kandahar that determined the rules under the Taliban.

Faruqi continued: "It's my business how long I keep my beard. It's not for someone to tell me to grow it this long or that long," stroking the end of a beard that it seemed would satisfy the most conservative Taliban. He also didn't like being told when to go to the mosque and when to pray: "I am a Muslim. I know when to pray. Sometimes they would come from Kandahar and tell us what the Quran says. I know what the Quran says."

Like our young escort, Faruqi also enjoyed his music, and one of the first things he had done when the Taliban were defeated was permit the music stores to reopen.

They were happy to see the backs of the Taliban.

But Surmad was located deep within Afghanistan's Pashtun belt, and like most people in the south and the east of the country, the men on the couch that day were not happy to see the Northern Alliance back in power, in the same capital they had destroyed when they last ruled Afghanistan.

In Surmad, people wanted only U.S. soldiers, and lots of them. "We need at least 50,000," Faruqi said. His friend chimed in: "No, we need 100,000." In those first few months after the Taliban's defeat, U.S. soldiers would have been welcomed as liberators in the Pashtun areas, the same areas where the Taliban had been strongest.

Faruqi and his friends weren't sophisticated men. They lived in

Afghanistan's backward hinterland, and on that day in December 2001, they believed the United States and the West could clean up the mess their country had become over the last two decades of endless war and repression. They believed the United States would free them from the brutal leaderships they had endured.

Faruqi lamented his poor country's recent past, his words tumbling out, as if his thoughts were moving too fast for his mouth. He was leaning so far forward it seemed he might fall off the couch. He expressed hope for an end to the bitter and relentless internecine fighting. He was just tired of it, and the only saviors he could see were the U.S. soldiers.

But the United States had other ideas. It had plans for its soldiers in Iraq. As a result, the United States took its guidance from Northern Alliance leaders who wanted only to regain control of Afghanistan. The United States deployed a force smaller than that of the New York City Police Department and handed Afghanistan over to Northern Alliance militiamen who had personal scores to settle with Pashtuns. The United States asked them to hunt the same al Qaeda men they had once harbored and gave Afghanistan's ethnic minorities a free pass to hunt down Pashtuns in the name of tracking Taliban. Within six months, most Pashtuns would blame the United States for bringing back warlords and criminals and for making every Pashtun a suspected Taliban.

At the heart of those misguided machinations was Zalmay Khalilzad, the U.S. president's hand-picked envoy to Afghanistan, who choreographed the early U.S. decisions that turned the country over to the Northern Alliance, alienated the Pashtun majority, and caused a lot of angry Pashtuns to realign themselves with whatever was left of the Taliban. As a result, a movement that was effectively dead in December 2001 would be resuscitated.

In those early days of victory, there was no sympathy, even within the United Nations, for Afghanistan's Pashtun majority, who were too afraid to speak out for fear they would be branded Taliban.

Khalilzad spoke both Persian and Pashtu. He was born in Afghanistan, got his university education both in Beirut and Chicago, became an American citizen, rose through the ranks of the Republican Party, headed George W. Bush's transition team for the Department of Defense, and in post-Taliban Afghanistan had Secretary of Defense Donald Rumsfeld's ear.

Khalilzad had also been in the State Department in the late 1980s, advising the undersecretary of state for political affairs on both the Soviet war in Afghanistan and the Iran-Iraq war. Those were the same years the United States pushed through a peace accord in Afghanistan and, in their haste to get out of Afghanistan, pressed feuding mujahedeen leaders into accords they signed and broke.

As point man in Afghanistan for both President Bush and Secretary Rumsfeld, Khalilzad made disastrous choices. He knew the men of the Northern Alliance, yet ignored their murderous history that had given rise to the Taliban; partnered them with U.S. soldiers; declared them the victorious army, although it was U.S. and British air power that had defeated the Taliban; treated Afghanistan as the spoils of war and handed the country to Northern Alliance leaders, who divided it up into fiefdoms; and then enlisted their militias in the hunt for al Qaeda and Taliban.

The Northern Alliance used U.S. soldiers to settle old scores, to intimidate and terrorize. Tribal enemies were turned in as Taliban. U.S. jets bombed villages and convoys wrongly identified by their Afghan allies as harboring al Qaeda and Taliban.

A frustrated U.S. marine commander who had to decide when to call in the bombers said he was put on the ground in Afghanistan without any solid intelligence, and with only a crude and unreliable means of verifying the intelligence he received:

> For five years we were not engaged here. We are coming in cold; our intelligence is zero. We don't know who is the bad guy and who is the good guy. We get a call from one of the Afghan commanders we work with who says that guy is a

Taliban or that convoy is a Taliban or al Qaeda convoy. But we don't know. We make a few checks. We call the [U.S.] embassy. We try to find out, but then we have to make a decision.

Some of them were wrong. Just one day before Hamid Karzai was to be sworn in as the first post-Taliban acting president, U.S. jets bombed a convoy of men heading to Kabul to congratulate him. The bombs blew apart several cars, killed twelve men and smashed into nearby mountain villages, killing another fifteen people.

In the convoy and among the dead were members of the Gardez *shura,* the equivalent of the Gardez municipal council. The attack on the convoy was part of a lethal power play for control of Gardez, not about either Taliban or al Qaeda.

But the U.S. soldiers on the ground didn't know that. They knew only what their supposed ally had told them.

The man they had been convinced by was Bacha Khan Zardran, a grotesque-looking mountain of a man with an oversized turban that stopped just above his copious eyebrows. An out-of-control mustache decorated his face, and his jowls fell in rolls that hid his thick neck. Zardran wanted Gardez and would later order a bloody assault, in which more than 800 rockets were fired, in a failed attempt to get it.

Zardran's men had blocked the main road to Kabul, forcing the convoy onto an obscure mountain road. Then they confronted their gullible U.S. allies, identifying the convoy as Taliban and al Qaeda men trying to sneak toward Kabul.

Hazrat Ali fingered his white beard nervously as he recalled the bombing. He had been in the convoy. His good friend Wali Marjan had died. "We weren't al Qaeda men. We were the Gardez *shura* and some members of our family. Bacha Khan's men told us we couldn't pass on the main road so we had to go another way. But it was difficult. The mountain passes were full of snow. We had to turn back. We heard planes overhead and we stopped. We waited maybe thirty minutes but there was no bombing. We started again."

Hazrat Ali, surrounded by several other members of the Gardez *shura* sitting nearby, paused. One of the other *shura* members continued: "We were all Taliban because we had to be. If you were a leader of your tribe, you were an official of the Taliban, you didn't have any choice," Naeem Koochi said.

When Hazrat Ali started talking again, his voice was hardly a whisper: "I heard the planes again, but this time the bombing began. I looked behind and Wali Marjan's car was gone, destroyed. I don't remember everything. I stopped the car and ran into the snow. The bombing went on and on. It lasted for hours." His voice trailed off. "Bacha Khan wanted us gone, but we're still here, some of us. Why does America listen to him?"

In another disastrous bombing raid in nearby Ghazni Province, a criminal named Mullah Wazeer, who had challenged the new Northern Alliance administration, was identified to U.S. Special Forces as a senior Taliban. But Mullah Wazeer was unknown to the Taliban.

His home was in the village of Peetra, tucked in the shadows of a barren mountain. Not long after the annual Muslim festival of Eid, while children were playing outside and twenty-nine-year-old Abdul Mohammed had just returned from Iran to find a bride, the U.S. planes appeared. There were two jets; they flew in low, pounding the area with bombs. The children were playing in a field, not far from Mullah Wazeer's house, which was empty. He had left two weeks earlier. The children had no time to hide. They died where they played: seven boys and two girls, all under the age of thirteen.

Abdul Mohammed was further away. He had been sent by his mother to get water. The bomb killed him instantly.

His mother, Aysha Bibi, goes often to his grave. Draped in a giant black shawl, she just sits and rocks in front of the spindly sticks on which brightly colored pieces of cloth fly, the only grave marking. Aysha Bibi is a widow. Her husband died in the 1980s anti-Soviet war, killed by Russian bombs.

An elder of Aysha Bibi's village, Maulvi Abdul Ghafoor, although a slight man with a white beard, has a voice that is thick with anger. He blamed the United States and said his village no longer wanted their help even with reconstruction: "We want them to leave. We don't want their help."

The graveyard was a short walk from the village. In the field outside Mullah Wazeer's house was a small memorial to the dead children. Nine small mounds of rocks mark where each child was last seen playing. Zarwar Khan's only two sons were killed in the attack. He stood by the graves, silent, his head bent. His brother, who had also lost one son, talked. Women had miscarried that day because of the bombing, he said.

An old man, the grandfather of several of the dead children, slowly, with a great deal of reverence, retrieved a dirty plastic bag from a bright green silk cloth. In the bag were small pieces of bones he believed belonged to his dead grandchildren. Gently, he returned them to the bag, rewrapped them in their green cloth, and said: "They are part of our memorial."

In Dah Rawood in southern Uruzgan Province, helicopter gunships attacked a wedding, after being told that senior Taliban were meeting there. But the wedding had been for a relative of a friend and supporter of Hamid Karzai. The scene was chaotic and bloody.

The helicopters hovered near the building where the women had gathered. Segregation even at weddings is common in conservative Afghanistan. When the firing began, the women and children ran from the building. They scattered, some headed into a nearby shed, others into an expanse of trees. Inside the helicopter gunship, the soldiers thought they were taking aim at fleeing Taliban. When the shooting stopped, forty-two people had been killed, most of them women and children. None among them were Taliban.

On the ground, most of the raids by U.S. soldiers and their Afghan allies were carried out in areas so remote that villagers had never seen a Westerner. Sometimes raids were conducted in the mountains, where shepherds ran at the sight of the deep green Apache helicopters with their gyrating propeller blades howling down on them.

A U.S. helicopter had landed on a hill near Gardez, and soldiers arrested three farmers who ran at the sight of it. The terrified shepherds were forced into the helicopter and taken to Bagram air base, where it was discovered that they had bolted not because they were insurgents but simply because the helicopter and soldiers had frightened them.

During such encounters, and usually unknown to nearby U.S. soldiers, Afghan militiamen rummaged through people's belongings, stole jewelry and money, and threatened to identify the people within as Taliban if they spoke out.

In southeastern Zabul Province, Abdullah, who was barely thirty-two years, cheered the day the Taliban disappeared. Then one day in late August 2002, several U.S. soldiers and dozens of Afghan militia raided his uncle's home. They herded the family into a dirt courtyard and forced them to sit there for the entire night. Inside, gold bangles were taken; his small cousin's gold earrings disappeared. Throughout the night, the women cried; the men stayed silent, afraid of being identified as Taliban and taken away. They had heard that the Americans took Afghans to some other country.

Within a year of the Taliban's defeat, the U.S. army, once welcomed as a liberator, was feared by ordinary Afghans. In rural Afghanistan, people no longer knew what the United States and its coalition partners were trying to do. Some had become convinced they had come to attack them because they were Muslims.

During those critical eighteen to twenty months following the collapse of the Taliban, when the West needed to engage and co-opt ethnic Pashtuns and bring the country's ethnic groups together, the schisms yawned ever wider. An opportunity was squandered as Northern Alliance militia sowed seeds of deeper discontent among the Pashtuns, and the United States and its coalition partners were seen as willing partners.

Zabul Province, which became a hotbed of Taliban resurgence

in 2004, had volunteered thousands of recruits to the new national Afghan army in those first months following the Taliban's collapse. A deputy police chief told me he had lineups of young men wanting to go to Kabul to become policemen. He sent several hundred, but most of them soon returned, humiliated and angry at the discrimination they suffered. The Northern Alliance leaders who vetted recruits toyed with the Pashtun recruits. Four men out of the hundreds who applied stuck it out. Most of the others joined the Taliban.

By the middle of 2002, frightened and disillusioned Pashtuns were ready to believe anything of the U.S. soldiers. Taliban hiding in the mountains took advantage of the discontent. They circulated Pashtu- and Persian-language posters that showed U.S. soldiers patting down Afghan women and girls. Beneath the pictures were admonishments to Muslims for allowing women to be mauled by men.

In late 2002 in a small village in southeastern Afghanistan, residents believed that the U.S. Special Forces who had come to search their homes for weapons wanted to kill them because they were Muslims. When they saw the soldiers approach, the eldest of the village took a white sheet and wrapped up a package that he hid in a dried riverbed. When the soldiers came and searched the village, they found the white package. Inside was the Quran, along with other Islamic icons.

The village elder spoke to the soldiers, his voice cracking with fear: "We thought that if you found out we were Muslim you would kill us."

In that first year or so, hundreds of Pashtuns were arrested. Anyone who had fought with the Taliban was branded a terrorist, yet they weren't. There had been conscription under the Taliban, and others who had willingly gone into battle believed they were fighting for their faith. Almost none were on the battlefield as part of a global jihad.

In northern Afghanistan, men were packed into cattle cars, so tightly crammed together that many suffocated and died. Those who survived were taken to Rashid Dostum's prison in Shebergan. Thousands were held there; some starved to death, others were slaughtered. Dostum was a key U.S. ally then.

Some in the jail were old men; others were children. They weren't fighting for world domination or to destroy the United States. They thought they were fighting for their country, their religion, their culture.

Anti-Taliban leaders like Dostum handed over men and boys to the United States, labeling them terrorists before they had even been questioned.

Mohammed Sanghir, a Pakistani Muslim missionary in his late fifties, was arrested in Afghanistan and spent more than one year in Guantanamo, the U.S.-run prison in Cuba, before being released. He had been in Afghanistan for three months before the September 11, 2001, attacks on the United States. As a devout Muslim, he sympathized with the Taliban's interpretation of Islam, but he had had no military training and had not fought with the Taliban. But he was in Kunduz when the Taliban collapsed and was taken to Dostum's Shebergan prison. He remembered the suffocating cattle car that nearly killed him.

For several months, he stayed in Dostum's jail. No one interrogated him. And then one day, without warning, he was sent to Kandahar and then to Guantanamo. Still no one had asked him anything.

Sanghir kept his Guantanamo identification bracelet on his thin wrist when he returned to Pakistan. "What did I do? I didn't know where they were taking me when they took me to Guantanamo. No one asked me any questions. I told everyone I was a *tableequi* [missionary]. I was only there to preach Islam. I was not a fighter. But I couldn't get anyone to listen, to understand."

Sanghir was among the first men taken to Guantanamo and one of the first to be released. In those first few weeks in Guantanamo, the restrictions were punishing. Men weren't allowed to pray, weren't allowed to read the Quran, and weren't allowed to talk. Men were shaved, contrary to Islamic tradition. The devout among them lived in fear of being fed pork, a forbidden food in Islam.

The United States also had a prison in Afghanistan, at Bagram, north of Kabul. In December 2002, two prisoners were beaten to death there. Access to the sprawling two-story prison compound at Bagram was closely guarded. A ten-foot-high external wall and coils of barbed wire on the ground surrounded the building. Sheet metal and wood slabs covered the windows.

Two prisoners, Saif-ur Rahman and Qayyum, both interviewed separately and unknown to each other, related similar accounts of their time in the U.S. prison at Bagram, of the abuses they endured. Both complained of sleep deprivation, of being forced to stand for long periods of time, of humiliating taunts from women soldiers who screamed abuse at them through closed doors.

Rahman and Qayyum were arrested in northeast Kunar: Rahman in December 2002 and Qayyum in August 2002. Qayyum was captured along with Hajji Ruhollah Wakil, the leader of a small Wahabi religious party. Rahman had been a big supporter of U.S. troops in Kunar and had fought against the Taliban. After their capture, the men were flown out of Kunar by helicopter, their hands tied and eyes blindfolded. Rahman's helicopter landed first in Jalalabad, where he was stripped, doused with ice water, and held for twenty-four hours.

His interrogators were two Americans who used dogs to frighten him. Rahman shook when he spoke of the dogs, their barking: "They were loud and so close to me. I tried not to move."

At Bagram, the prisoners were given red suits, along with two blankets and a carpet on which to sleep. The lights were always on, and prisoners were allowed to wash only once a week for five minutes. Qayyum was questioned there in a second-floor room, always led there with his head hooded and his hands handcuffed.

Both men said they were threatened with being sent to Guantanamo. "One of them [interrogators] brought me fifty small stones and said, 'Count these stones.' When I finished, he said,

'We will send you there [Guantanamo] for fifty years,'" remembered Rahman.

Rahman also said, "I was sad because I was the enemy of al Qaeda and Taliban. I was not the criminal. I fought the Taliban." After the Taliban's fall, Rahman and his brother, Malik Zareen, a prominent commander in the U.S.-allied Northern Alliance, seized control of Kunar for the allies in their war on terror.

Rahman was embarrassed to say U.S. forces had arrested him: "I tell everyone I was in Kabul to visit Karzai. I don't tell anyone I was in Bagram. They would laugh at me. At Bagram, Taliban prisoners would shout at me, 'These are your friends. This is what happens to friends of the Americans.'"

Saif-ur Rahman was embarrassed to speak of his ordeal. He looked away; his eyes were closed as he told of his nakedness, about how he was forced to lie spread-eagle on the dirt floor with his hands palm up so his interrogators could position the legs of a chair on his open palms and feet, sometimes applying pressure by sitting or putting their feet on the chair. Rahman was in handcuffs for twenty days, even at mealtimes.

Qayyum said he was held in a large hall with around 100 other prisoners. There were ten people to a cubicle, cordoned off from other similar cubicles by sheets of mesh. He was held for two months and five days, and throughout that time he was forbidden to talk to his cell mates.

When they were released, both men said their American captors told them: "We are here to help you. The Taliban and al Qaeda are your enemy. They destroyed your country."

But they no longer believed them.

The heavy-handed brutality was not restricted to Bagram. I had heard of other abuses by U.S. and coalition soldiers, some of the worst from an Afghan friend, whom I referred to as Bibi Jan, which means "dear aunt," when she requested that I keep her real name discreet.

She is a diminutive woman, with short-cropped hair and a round and open face. In late summer 2002, when we spoke about the complaints she had investigated, she was afraid. Bibi Jan was a woman who was not easily cowed, but this time she was reluctant to talk and afraid to be identified. We had spoken often, and her criticism of the warlords who replaced the Taliban was stinging.

When I saw her, she was holding a brown folder that concealed dozens of papers, handwritten notes, details of abuses by U.S. soldiers and their Afghan militia allies. The type and extent of the abuses dismayed her. She had eyewitness accounts and documentation that she wanted to give to Hamid Karzai.

In her office, she told me of some of the abuses: "But please don't use my name again. The last time I got into so much trouble." Bibi Jan was referring to the death threats she had received and to the intimidating nighttime raids by police, made because she had attacked the powerful warlords, such men as the former defense minister Fahim, and Abdul Rasul Sayyaf.

This time, her information accused the U.S. military, and she was having trouble getting her president to listen. She wanted Karzai to talk to the Americans, explain the people's shame at some of their tactics and anger at others. She wanted him to tell the Americans to stop, to understand that they were alienating people who wanted to be their friends.

Her report was thick with evidence. One of the complaints had come from Ghazni Province. U.S. Special Forces soldiers were looking for a Taliban leader, and they were told some of the local people might have information.

A tent was erected on a desolate stretch of land. Several villagers were called inside the tent. They sat on the ground, pressing against the walls of the tent, in the middle of which was a chair. U.S. soldiers brought a man into the tent, forced him to strip naked, and sat him in the chair. He was forced to bend over, and his hands were tied to his ankles. Bibi Jan leaned forward to demonstrate.

"He was humiliated and every Afghan there was humiliated. They will never find anyone like that. I want the president to talk to them, make them understand that they shouldn't treat our people like that."

Soldiers kept their captive in that position while he was questioned. Eventually, he was released. There were other examples, Bibi Jan said. She selected one paper that told of dogs being used to threaten and frighten prisoners; and another that told of women soldiers teasing and hurling abuses at men, whom they made strip, of homes ransacked and looted by the Afghan militia who accompanied the special forces; and so it went on.

In the south and the east of Afghanistan, the West watched and even abetted as Pashtuns were marginalized, intimidated, and harassed. This crippled coalition efforts to find al Qaeda holdouts, and it breathed life into a dying Taliban movement.

The disappointment and disillusionment spread, and by September 2004, the United States had had its reputation besmirched even in the heartland of the Northern Alliance. At a ceremony in the Panjshir Valley to mark the third anniversary of the death of Ahmed Shah Massood, known as the Lion of the Panjshir, the dirt road that led up the valley was protected by a massive iron gate. On each side of the entrance, there were paintings of lions that failed to capture the ferociousness the artist was surely seeking. Instead, the lions seemed to smile and looked as if they had been drawn from a children's coloring book.

Three young men with guns stood by, protected from the wind by a tattered canvas shelter that also housed a battered wooden table and a collection of old Russian helmets. Nearby, the green water of the Panjshir River charged noisily over the rocky riverbed, flanked by the Hindu Kush Mountains.

The young soldiers standing guard spoke of their disappointment with the new leadership in Afghanistan. But their bitterest criticism was for the United States. They had expected more from a new Afghanistan.

"Nothing has changed. We have nothing, and I am not sure I have any hope anymore," said Darya Khan, a slight man with a clean-shaven face and deep brown eyes, who cradled a cigarette in his hands. He had been with Massood in the Panjshir Valley during the five years that the Taliban ruled Kabul. "We thought when the Americans and everyone came things would be different, better. But it's not. It's the same. And there is still fighting."

Massood's Panjshir Valley looked much the same as the Pashtun south and east. Women wore burqas. Through the dusty haze, horse-drawn carriages clopped down the rocky roads, carrying female passengers huddled close together and hidden beneath their burqas. Massood's home village of Bazarak was tucked into the mountainside, and the homes were a collection of cement or mud, baked in the searing sun. A few small tea stalls and rickety shops lined the only street.

I stayed with Massood's father-in-law, Tajuddin. At a crumbling tea house across the street from Tajuddin's home, several men grumbled. The walls of the tea house were barren but for the streaks of dirt and two red carpets attached with big steel hooks. It was a traditional tea house where you sipped sweet green tea atop carpeted tables. In one corner, four grizzled old men talked and drank tea. Smoke from their cigarettes wafted across the early morning rays of sun that burst through the only window, crudely cut into the wall of the cement building. Flies played on the flat unleavened bread as we listened to the misgivings of the men who had been Massood's neighbors. They had welcomed the United States three years ago. Now they, too, wanted them to leave.

"They are the problem now," said Rehmat Beg, who had been a mujahedeen fighter with Massood. "The Taliban are gone now. We wanted them to come and to help us get rid of them, but we don't want them here now."

Beg grumbled that northern Afghanistan had not received enough from the post-Taliban administration. He was unhappy with the Afghan government, including the Panjshiris. Pretending to put money in his chest pocket, Beg said: "All the government people just put money in their pockets. The Americans take our money, too. We have heard that American soldiers steal from our homes, insult our women."

One of the men accused the U.S. soldiers of stealing young Afghan girls. "They wait outside the schools and take them. They don't understand our culture, our traditions. They should leave."

CHAPTER EIGHT

The Hidden Face of Pakistan's Military

Historically, the United States and Pakistan have either loathed or loved each other. Their relationship has been like a long and turbulent marriage, with a courtship initiated not long after the end of World War II and the beginning of the Cold War.

The United States was looking for allies to girdle a burgeoning Soviet empire that was already bulging into the Asian subcontinent and Pakistan was a newly created country ripped from a larger India in the waning years of the British Empire. Pakistan wanted the threat of U.S. muscle against an independent India that it now saw as its enemy.

But history has not been kind to Pakistan, whose birth in 1947 as a homeland for greater India's dispossessed Muslims was difficult and bloody. The dead numbered in the millions. Tortured memories still haunt the generation that lived through that turbulence: rampaging mobs setting entire streets on fire, running throughout the night with a bloodlust that couldn't be quenched; ghost trains chugging across the new frontier, carrying charred corpses, the victims of the rioting mobs; children being grabbed from their beds by frightened parents who dragged them from one hiding place to another, sleeping by day, walking throughout the night. Hindu hordes slaughtered Muslims in India, and in the new Pakistan, Muslim mobs carried out ferocious massacres of Hindus.

The hero of Pakistan's independence movement, Mohammed Ali Jinnah, a gaunt, lanky man who died of tuberculosis just two years after Pakistan was created, paled against India's Mahatma Gandhi, the spindly legged pacifist with the wire-rimmed spectacles whose campaign of peaceful civil disobedience created a firestorm of national pride that forced Britain out of the subcontinent.

Unsure how to make a graceful exit, Britain let Muslims and Hindus decide. Those regions of India dominated by Muslims became Pakistan. But there were anomalies: East Pakistan, which would later become Bangladesh, was given over to the new country, despite being separated from West Pakistan by thousands of kilometers. Hyderabad, smack in the middle of India, was kept by Hindu India despite being overwhelmingly Muslim. And Kashmir, the former princely state, was mostly Muslim but ruled by a Hindu king. India kept it after the king refused to let the Muslim majority vote. And in 1948, before the ink on their independence papers had even had a chance to dry, the two countries had found the grounds to fight their first war.

Pakistan emerged a confusing and conflicted mix of ethnic groups with little in common but their religion. Brawny Pashtun warriors lived in the northwest. In the Punjab, people were smaller, farmed the fertile plains, and lived as indentured slaves to powerful landowners. In that respect, Punjabis and those living in Pakistan's southern Sindh Province were similar: slaves to big landlords, created by the departing British, who rewarded a small number of their Muslim stalwarts with vast chunks of the newly created nation. Those powerful feudal landowners took over from the British as the new rulers of Pakistan.

But they weren't alone. Pakistan inherited military men, because in British India, the military was just about the only place a Muslim could find a good job. Muslims had trouble getting a job in Britain's colonial administration, which favored Hindus who had been at the bottom of the heap during the glory days of the Muslim Mogul Empire. Hindus dominated the courts, the government, banks, and British-run industries. Muslims, having to look elsewhere for work, found it in the military.

And so when the British departed, they left behind a newly created Pakistan that had only its Islamic religion to bind it and a ruling class of either feudal or military men who had neither the ability nor the desire to create the free and fair institutions and the administration that could develop democratic governance in Pakistan. The most influential families in Pakistan sought only to monopolize power, and to this end, they put their sons both in the military and in politics.

The new Pakistani army officers spoke English, wore the cravat at social functions, sipped black tea, and drank sherry. But not everything was as it had been under the British.

Fear of India consumed Pakistan in those first years after independence, and the Pakistani drill sergeants weren't motivating their young recruits with talk of king and country but with ideas of jihad and country.

An old friend of mine, a retired army general, once told me that the link between jihad and the Pakistan military is as old as the Pakistan army:

> I remember giving a talk to the troops of my tank unit as far back as 1962 on the concept of jihad. Jihad has always been a motivating concept for our troops since day one. This was done because the principal enemy was India, a non-Muslim state. Religion has been an important factor in the military, but there are a couple of landmarks that explain the progression.

The first was the 1948 war over Kashmir. Pakistan was still stinging from India's refusal to hand over the territory at independence. Emotions were raw, but the rawest were among the conservative Pashtun tribesmen in Pakistan's frontier province, hundreds of kilometers away. They held tribal *jirgas,* and for hours, sometimes days, the elders sat, sipped tea, and deplored India's refusal to hand over Kashmir. They waited for the Kashmiris to revolt, and when that didn't happen, they marched to liberate the Muslim Kashmiris from Indian rule.

"They were a volunteer army, the very first use of mujahedeen. It was very early in our history," my friend told me.

Pakistan lost the war. There was a handful of regular army officers sprinkled among the tribesmen, whose military campaign disintegrated into an orgy of looting and plundering.

They never did capture Srinagar, Kashmir's summer capital and the sanctuary for the rich fleeing India's brutal summer heat, and eventually a peace agreement was reached that divided Kashmir between Pakistan and India. The division was supposed to be temporary to let tempers cool before the two countries worked out an agreement.

Both sides still struggle to work out that agreement more than half a century later, and tempers on both sides of the divide still routinely run hot.

In that 1948 scrimmage, Islam was used as the banner under which the war was waged. For Pakistan, it was a defining moment that cemented the relationship between the military and religion.

Yet Pakistan's army still embraced British traditions. No one seemed to see a contradiction between using jihad to motivate the troops while sitting in the spotless mess halls talking strategy over a glass of whiskey. As my friend the general put it: "When I joined in 1961, drinking and dancing was the done thing in the military, but even then there were people who were religious. Not many officers prayed five times. We only went for Jumma [Friday] prayers, usually with the troops in the unit mosque."

By then, Pakistan's military was cozying up to the United States, the newest superpower. India with its socialist roots and its chauvinistic nationalism had forged strong ties with the Soviet

Union, the other superpower. The respective spheres of influence were becoming defined.

While many Pakistani army officers still trained at Britain's Royal Military Academy at Sandhurst and British traditions ran deep in the Pakistan military, a new generation of soldiers was also heading further west, traveling to the United States for training.

By the late 1950s and early 1960s, Britain had already lost much of its luster; it was an empire on the decline and a former colonial ruler. As the general put it: "Many Pakistanis also felt that the problems between India and Pakistan were a legacy of the British. But more than any other reason was the growing power of the Americans and the waning of the British Empire. We were drawn to the bigger power, especially the one who was not our colonial ruler."

Pakistan joined U.S.-orchestrated Cold War alliances. It signed up for the Southeast Asia Treaty Organization (SEATO) in 1954, created to oppose further Communist gains in Southeast Asia. The next year, Pakistan signed on to the Central Treaty Organization (CENTO), probably the least successful of the Cold War alliances, with promises of U.S. military and economic aid. Intended to resemble NATO, the goal of this alliance that also included Turkey, Iraq, and Iran was to contain communism by lining up strongly pro-U.S. states along the underbelly of the Soviet Union.

Pakistan began to import its military hardware from the United States, including the Patton tanks that Pakistan used in its wars against India. Pakistan also got F-86 Saber jets, those bulbous 1950s fighter aircraft that roared onto black-and-white movie screens, blasting away at the hulking Godzilla. The relationship between Pakistan and the United States hummed along until 1965, when war broke out for the second time against India.

On September 6, Farooq Adam was on the front lines, a young army officer, trained at Sandhurst like his father before him. He had enlisted just four years earlier. The fighting was brutal; the barrages were relentless, and in just two weeks Pakistan had run through all its artillery and tank ammunition. The soldiers sought replacement supplies. They waited, hunkered down in trenches, husbanding the ammunition they still had. Despite all the alliances, they waited in vain.

Adam, who came home from that war a decorated soldier, said Pakistan was betrayed by the United States. As part of the CENTO alliance, Pakistan was dependent on the United States for both its hardware and its ammunition. The war had devastated its supplies, and the United States refused to send fresh supplies and warned the other members of CENTO not to supply Pakistan. CENTO was set up to contain the Soviet Union and the United States was unwilling to get involved in volatile South Asia.

The relationship between Pakistan and the United States would never recover. Pakistan would never again completely trust the United States or see it as a guarantor of its safety: "By then we were totally equipped by the Americans through CENTO; we had a military alliance with them. All our replacement had to come through the Americans. They stopped all our ammunition, and instead of helping us they stopped even our other allies from helping us."

Turkey and Iran, also partners in the CENTO alliance, surreptitiously exported supplies into Pakistan. But it wasn't enough, and on September 23, just seventeen days after the war began, Pakistan was defeated. As Adam put it: "The Americans were a lost cause to us in 1965. When we really needed them in 1965, they weren't there. They didn't help us. But our defeat in 1965 didn't compare to the shame of the 1971 war."

The 1971 war was Pakistan's third war against India and was its most humiliating military defeat. It cost Pakistan a significant portion of its territory and devastated its national pride. The aftermath was disastrous.

Nearly 100,000 Pakistani soldiers were taken as prisoners of war by India; Bangladesh emerged from the ashes of East Pakistan as an independent country; the war churned up a venom within the military toward Pakistan's military and political leadership, whom it blamed for the defeat; and for a second time, Pakistan was disappointed with the United States for failing to come to its aid. And most important, it turned a demoralized military toward its Islamic roots, particularly those among the military who believed they had failed forcefully to defend the religion that had been the reason for Pakistan's creation nearly a quarter of a century earlier.

The 1971 war lasted just twenty-three days before Pakistan's military commander, Lieutenant General Amir Abdullah Khan Niazi, surrendered.

"The anger I felt, I wept like a bloody child, the sheer disgrace, the sheer loss of honor, the manner of our defeat," remembered Adam, who received the commander in chief's commendation for gallantry because he deserted his teaching job at the Pakistan Military Academy to join his unit on the front line against India: "Just think of it—I had this cushy, safe job but I just walked off. I didn't tell anyone. I just left and joined my unit."

Again Pakistan waited for U.S. help. This time it pinned its hopes on the Seventh Fleet, which Washington had threatened to send in if India crossed its borders. But once more, American support never arrived.

Adam was not surprised: "We didn't expect anything of the United States after 1965, but our anger was directed at our own military leadership, the corruption, the cowardice." He added that President General Pervez Musharraf, a junior officer in 1971 and a member of the Pakistani equivalent of the Green Berets, "was just as angry as I was."

Adam's anger festered, and he decided to stage a coup to get rid of the military leadership and with it the civilian president, Zulfikar Ali Bhutto, a populist leader who would roll up his sleeves and scream slogans to the country's poor, promising them bread, clothes, and housing.

It was a blistering hot June day in 1972 when the idea to stage a coup germinated in Adam's mind. He had gone home to see his newborn daughter, and as always, talk turned to politics and the military debacle. Among the men at the table were retired generals, "and I just hypothetically said what was required for this country was a benevolent dictator to set things right, that we had a moral obligation to set it right."

Inside the small bus that Adam boarded to return to his barracks, the sun's rays bore down on him and his mind wandered. "My mind kept thinking about a coup and I started thinking in my mind how to organize one. I even had a code word. It would be 'black dog barking,' and the reply would be, 'he requires a white horse.'" Adam chose both black dog and white horse because they referred to whiskey brands.

Over the next seven months, Adam and a handful of friends began recruiting for their coup, which would become known as the Attock Conspiracy case, named for the medieval Attock Fort where the coup conspirators would be tried and jailed.

The coup was set for August 1973. But in March, one of the co-conspirators was caught when he mistakenly revealed the plan.

Bhutto was told of the coup plot and ordered several officers to infiltrate Adam's cabal. At 3 A.M. on March 3, 1973, military police pounded on the young army major's door, slapped ankle chains on him, and hauled him off to prison.

Some fifty-five officers were arrested in the failed coup attempt. Fifteen were air force officers, the rest were army men. Twenty-three men went on trial; fifteen were sent to jail. Adam received the heaviest sentence—ten years.

Musharraf was a junior officer when Adam went to jail. Adam said, "I can tell you that he and his type of officers would have had a lot of sympathy for us. We were all angry. It didn't matter whether you were liberal or religious."

But things just got worse for Pakistan.

In 1974, India detonated a nuclear device. The explosion ripped a giant hole in Pakistan's national pride, still ravaged by its 1971 defeat. Its prisoners of war had just returned home after two years in Indian captivity; there was widespread grumbling inside Pakistan that the United States couldn't be trusted as a military ally; and the military balance had dramatically shifted in India's favor with the nuclear explosion.

Bhutto was at the airport in Lahore when word reached him of the nuclear test. He vowed then that Pakistan would build a nuclear device. That same day, he made a televised promise to the Pakistani nation: "Pakistanis will eat grass, but we will have the bomb."

Adam summed up the effect of Bhutto's promise:

> Zulfikar Ali Bhutto was so popular when he said those words on television. We were a defeated nation and we didn't know what India could do to us. We thought they could destroy us. The nuclear bomb for us was a natural thing. We knew we couldn't rely on the United States to protect us; our nuclear bomb was a consequence of the total lack of faith that the Pakistan army and the Pakistani people had in the American word. We were not going ever again to depend on the Americans to protect us.

Bhutto, who saw himself as a socialist revolutionary, and not a particularly religious man, sought to rebuild his country's shattered pride with anti-Indian and pan-Islamic slogans. Bhutto liberally used the slogans of Islam to reach Pakistan's poor and lower middle class, who became the underpinnings of his party's support. He emphasized Pakistan's Middle Eastern heritage and broke with Western alliances, pulling Pakistan out of the Commonwealth and SEATO. Bhutto was the first Pakistani leader to reach out to the poor, using Islam to sell them on his idea of Islamic socialism. He nationalized Pakistan's industries and private institutions.

But Bhutto wasn't the only one using Islam to reinvigorate a flagging nation. The religious right was also active, and by the early 1970s, Bhutto was under pressure from religious groups who used microphones mounted on the tens of thousands of mosques throughout Pakistan to galvanize the poor behind their Islamic sloganeering.

Bhutto moved quietly to appease, increasing the Islamic content in the school curriculum. Under pressure from Islamic groups at home and in Saudi Arabia, Bhutto changed the constitution and, in a symbolic gesture to conservative Islam, declared as non-Muslims a small minority sect known as Ahmedis. Reviled as heretics by mainstream Muslims because of their belief in a savior, Ahmedis were prevented from going to Mecca by the Saudi Arabians to perform the Muslim pilgrimage of Hajj, one of the five pillars of Islam.

During the Islamic revivalism of the 1970s, the Pakistani army began to change. Several officers recruited from Pakistan's elite private schools and trained at Sandhurst left after the 1971 defeat; new recruits from Pakistan's more conservative schools had begun to arrive. One instructor at the Pakistan Military Academy said that even as early as 1968, the complexion of the officer corps was changing, and instead of drawing officers from the country's elite, they were coming in from the middle and lower middle classes. The backgrounds of these officers were more orthodox and religious. "A preponderance of these basic madrassa school type of boys joined the army and kept creeping up the armed forces ladder," Adam said.

In 1975, Bhutto searched out the vacationing A. Q. Khan, a German-educated metallurgist, to head Pakistan's nuclear weapons program. Khan had been employed at a Dutch firm that subcontracted for a consortium specializing in the manufacture of nuclear equipment. Khan returned to the Netherlands at the end of his vacation, stole the German G2 centrifuge design, resigned, and returned home to Pakistan.

He was put to work by the Pakistan government, with money from Muammar Ghadaffi's Libya, to develop Pakistan's nuclear bomb.

On April 1, 1976, Bhutto made a surprise appointment of General Zia-ul Haq as army chief of staff, passing over five more senior generals to give Zia the job. A square-shouldered man with severe eyes set deep beneath a protruding forehead and surrounded by dark black circles, Zia was thought by Bhutto to be a malleable choice, a simple man who showed no outward signs of ambition and seemed more interested in his religious rituals than the politics of Pakistan. It proved to be Bhutto's biggest mistake.

Born in 1924 in Jalandher in India, Zia went to school in Delhi and served in British India's army, but when Pakistan became an independent country, he joined the Pakistan army. He believed deeply in Pakistan as a homeland for the subcontinent's Muslims. Zia trained at the U.S. Commander and Staff College in 1963, and from 1966 to 1970, he was in Jordan where he trained Jordanian soldiers.

One of his first acts as Pakistan's new army chief was to make religion the centerpiece, and for the first time, meetings and conferences were interrupted for prayers. Zia introduced a new motto for the army with faith and jihad at its heart. Soldiers were told they were soldiers of Islam.

Zia set a new standard for promotion of officers that put professionalism secondary to religious devotion. This policy sidelined some of the more secular officers and promoted the radical Islamists up the ranks.

Zia made the Quran compulsory learning material at staff colleges, and religious political literature was added to army training courses. Radical Islamist ideology began to permeate the military, and the influence of the most extreme groups crept into the army.

The most prominent among them was the Tableeqi Jamaat, an organization of Islamic missionaries who espoused an Islam that followed the literal interpretation of the Quran and required its adherents to follow the traditions of seventh-century Islam. Soldiers were encouraged to go to Tableeqi gatherings, the purpose of which was to indoctrinate the young cadets.

For Bhutto, politics began to sour soon after general elections in Pakistan in 1975. The religious right formed the Pakistan National Alliance to gang up against him, accusing him of vote rigging.

Bhutto didn't see it, but behind the Pakistan National Alliance was a disgruntled military, led by Zia, who had thrown together the alliance with the connivance of the strongest Islamic party, Jamaat-e-Islami (Party of Islam) and a smaller, but rigidly conservative, Jamiat-e-Ulema Islam (Party of Islamic Clerics).

Jamaat-e-Islami was the smartest and best organized of Pakistan's religious parties and as early as 1970 sent its followers, all of them hard-line Islamists, into the army and into the bureaucracy to burrow unnoticed deep within Pakistani society.

Bhutto tried to stem the tide by making concessions to the alliance. He outlawed alcohol and changed Pakistan's weekly day of rest from Sunday to Friday.

Until then, the rise of religious tendencies in the military had not directly affected the officer corps. They were still required to enter the messes clean-shaven, wearing a smartly pressed suit. My old friend the retired general told me: "We in the military were not happy with this decision, especially when it was not based on conviction but expediency and we knew that. The officers missed the booze in the mess, and now they had to drink in their homes."

Another retired army general and former head of the ISI, Hamid Gul, said Bhutto was like a man trying to row backward away from a raging waterfall. But he was trapped in the current.

On July 5, 1977, Zia staged his coup, arrested Bhutto, and promised elections within ninety days. He even freed Bhutto. But the populist leader was belligerent. He vowed to return to power and throw Zia and his coup leaders in jail. Instead, Zia threw him back in jail, orchestrated a murder case against him, sentenced him to die, and hanged him on April 6, 1979.

Adam, who was still in jail serving out his ten-year sentence, appealed to Zia for an early pardon. "I wrote a letter and said you should let me out because I am here for failing to do what you have done." Zia released him.

The world was outraged by Bhutto's hanging. Zia had ignored pleas from across the globe to spare Bhutto's life. The United States stopped all military and economic aid to Pakistan; Zia was declared a political villain in the United States. Relations between the two countries couldn't have been worse. But the Cold War was still on, and in December 1979, the Soviet Union invaded neighboring Afghanistan.

Ronald Reagan's newly installed administration saw the Soviet invasion as an attempt by Moscow to reach the Arabian Sea and a warm-water port. The United States turned to Pakistan, forgave the hanging of Bhutto, and embraced Zia.

My old friend the general, who attended some of those first meetings between Zia and the U.S. administration, said:

The government of Pakistan expressed its fear of the red storm rising, the czarist dream of moving toward the warm waters through Afghanistan and Pakistan; almost concurrently the United States also expressed its dissatisfaction with the Soviet invasion. All this happened almost as soon as the Soviets rolled into Afghanistan. This was the time when U.S. and Pakistani relations were at their lowest ebb. The Soviet invasion changed this. The United States made an initial $100-million military aid offer to Zia, who called it peanuts. I know all of this because I sat in on the first and the second set of meetings in Washington.

The United States upped the ante, and an alliance was born. Afghanistan's anti-Soviet fighters were called mujahedeen—holy warriors—and their war a jihad or holy war.

"Training camps were set up jointly by Pakistan and the United States to train mujahedeen leaders. Gulbuddin Hekmatyar, who by 2004 was defined as a terrorist, and Ahmed Shah Massood went through these training camps," my friend told me. The camps were structured. A Pakistani major in the Special Services Group, the same commando unit with which Musharraf had trained, was paired with an American officer, and together they made up a training team. It was through these team leadership units that military equipment and weapons were supplied to the mujahedeen.

Within two years of the Soviet invasion, Pakistan had millions of Afghan refugees in camps on its frontier. The majority were ethnic Pashtuns, like the Pakistanis of the frontier, and they were mostly rural and conservative. Afghanistan's urban population stayed at home because the cities still functioned under the protection of the Soviet soldiers. In rural areas, it was a different story: The countryside was being hit hard by Soviet fighter jets pounding villages to deny support to the mujahedeen, driving millions to the safety of Pakistan and Iran.

Tens of thousands of young fighting men were needed to fight the Soviet Goliath. Pakistan went looking for recruits in its religious schools. "With the support of the ISI and the knowledge of the U.S., the madrassas, especially the ones in the frontier went into action to produce mujahedeen, now called jihadis," said my friend.

While the United States was the biggest backer of the mujahedeen, it publicly maintained a strategy of "plausible denial." A close associate of Zia's, who throughout the 1980s war had been an intimate partner in U.S. negotiations, said:

> The impression that was being given was that it was the Afghans who were fighting the jihad. Of course the world knew better. The ISI became the active conduit for the funds, arms, and ammunition for the mujahedeen. It was a mega conduit. The United States even paid for arms supplied by other countries, including Pakistan.
>
> The American CIA and the ISI were as thick as thieves. Cooperation was in the supply of arms and ammunition and also training, especially in the initial phases. There was also cooperation in the field of intelligence. I am not sure, but the CIA paid for the arms and ammunition from Egypt. They did pay for the ammunition supplied by Pakistan. I know of some payments. The boss of the CIA regularly flew in to meet with Zia. I particularly remember [Bill] Casey.
>
> For the jihad in Afghanistan, against the Soviets, the CIA and ISI were two strands of one thread.

Early in 1980, Abdullah Azam, a Palestinian and mentor of Osama bin Laden, came to Pakistan to lead a recruitment drive to bring Middle Eastern youths to the Afghan jihad. Bin Laden worked with Azam at what was called the Services Center in Pakistan's frontier province, and together they churned out literature to entice disgruntled Middle Eastern men to Afghanistan.

Zia gave them Pakistani travel documents. They were trained in the camps run jointly by the United States and Pakistan. The U.S. money and ammunition was sent to the Afghan resistance through Pakistan.

The United States also pumped out inspirational literature of its own for the Afghan refugee camps, where U.S.-printed school books taught the alphabet by using such examples as: J is for Jihad, and K is for Kalashnikov, and I is for infidel. Mathematical problems would be something like: "If you had fifty Communist soldiers and you killed ten, how many would you still have?"

While the Afghan campaign forged ahead, sustained by Islamic fervor, Zia was active at home in Pakistan using Islam to consolidate his power. At the same time, President Ronald Reagan was publicly declaring Zia a champion of the free world. The United States ignored Zia's drive to turn his society into an Islamic one, and for the first time in Pakistan's history, Islamists moved into important government positions.

Zia introduced sweeping changes to Pakistan's legal system, setting up Shariat courts, which were established to try cases under Islamic law. Islamic legislation was introduced. The Hadood Ordinance became law in Pakistan, making it mandatory for women to find four male Muslims to witness a rape to get a conviction.

Zia set about introducing an Islamic banking system that would make interest collection illegal, and in June 1980, Zia gave the government the right to go into private bank accounts of its citizens to deduct the religious tax of Zakat, which was 2.5 percent of a person's annual income. Using some of this tax, tens of thousands of religious madrassas were created during Zia's eleven-year rule.

Afghan mujahedeen leaders such as Abdul Rasul Sayyaf were allowed to set up "universities" in the frontier, where men from across the world could train, men who eventually returned to such places as the Philippines, where the Abu Sayyaf group became established, and Indonesia, where Jamaah Islamiya would thrive, and Egypt, where al-Gamma al Islamiyya would churn out militant extremists. They would keep their ties to Pakistan's intelligence agency, which helped to spawn them.

Throughout the 1980s, Zia's military also forged ahead with its nuclear program, ignored by the United States. In 1981, despite growing worries over Pakistan's nuclear program, President Reagan lifted sanctions that had been imposed in the 1970s after Pakistan was caught smuggling uranium enrichment technology. In 1985, the U.S. Congress passed an amendment authored by former U.S. senator Larry Pressler requiring economic sanctions against Pakistan unless the White House could certify that Pakistan had not embarked on a nuclear weapons program. U.S. presidents certified this every year until 1990. Yet a declassified State Department memo from 1983 said Pakistan clearly had a nuclear weapons program that relied on stolen European technology.

By the late 1980s, the rumblings of a political revival had begun. Benazir Bhutto, the young daughter of Zulfikar Ali Bhutto, returned to Pakistan in 1986 to a gathering of more than 1 million people who overwhelmed the eastern city of Lahore to greet her.

Zia made some gratuitous political changes, holding non-party elections and setting up a parliament in 1985 that answered to him. When its prime minister, Mohammed Khan Junejo, a soft-spoken gentleman from southern Sindh, began to show signs of independence, Zia got rid of him.

Zia died in a mysterious plane crash in 1988, by which time the war in Afghanistan was winding down. Mikhail Gorbachev had called Afghanistan a bleeding wound and was negotiating the Soviet withdrawal.

Hamid Gul was head of Pakistan's ISI in those last years of the

Afghan war. A diminutive man with graying brown hair, who was among Pakistan's secret service men who recruited radical militants, Gul orchestrated the last big mujahedeen battle outside Jalalabad in eastern Afghanistan in February 1989, just days after the last Soviet soldier returned home on February 15.

Madrassa students from across Pakistan, most of them still in their teens, signed up to fight; they were filled with an urgency to wage jihad before it was over. The United States and Pakistan expected Afghanistan's Communist government to collapse quickly without Soviet backing to prop it up.

Osama bin Laden was on the battlefield along with hundreds of other Arab fighters. But the Communist government in Kabul held on without the Soviet Union. The United States began to pack its bags.

By 1990, Benazir Bhutto had been elected prime minister and a new army chief, General Mirza Aslam Beg, had been installed.

Only then, in 1990, after the Soviet Union had left Afghanistan and the Cold War had ended, did the United States remember Pakistan's nuclear program. It imposed sweeping sanctions, cutting off all military and humanitarian aid to Pakistan.

The sanctions hurt the military deeply. Already distrustful of a United States that had let it down both in 1965 and 1971, for Pakistan's military men it was confirmation of America's arrogance and indifference. As Gul recalled: "The sanctions changed the military's predisposition to the United States quite a bit. Sanctions came without a clear explanation. It didn't make sense that Pakistan had been its ally when the Communists were in Afghanistan and now they were suddenly targets of sanctions. There wasn't even an attempt at subtle disengagement."

The sanctions were all-encompassing; they ended the exchange of army officers between Pakistan and the United States, and Washington lost touch with an entire generation of new army officers. The 1990 sanctions came just as military rule ended in Pakistan and the first tentative and painfully wobbly steps toward democratic rule were being taken.

It wasn't a shining example of democracy at work. Benazir Bhutto was elected without any experience; the military pulled her strings; her ministers were corrupt and feudal, many of them made wealthy by collaboration with the military.

The new army chief, the barrel-chested General Mirza Aslam Beg, was openly hostile to the United States, and when the first Gulf War was brewing, he rebuffed U.S. requests for Pakistan to join the coalition against Iraq.

So, unexpectedly after a decade of U.S.-funded growth, the 1990s began badly for Pakistan. It was isolated, bereft of funding for its army and its nuclear program. Beg went looking for new friends and found them in Iran and China.

Iranian government representatives came to Pakistan the first time in late 1989 seeking nuclear expertise. They went straight to Beg. Three Iranians made that first trip to hold secret meetings. They wanted nuclear weapons technology and said they were ready to pay as much as $10 billion for it. Officially, Beg said that the Iranian delegation was in Pakistan to talk about reviving trade between the two countries. But the only thing the Iranians wanted to talk about was nuclear technology.

The first round of negotiations began while Benazir Bhutto was in power. Beg said the two played a cat-and-mouse game with the Iranian buyers, but never said no.

By August 1990, just twenty months since she took power, the military was tiring of Benazir Bhutto. She had sought to rein in the military, put it under civilian control. The army ordered the president, Ghulam Ishaq Khan, to use his constitutional powers to fire her. Khan, a career bureaucrat who had thrived under Zia, did the military's bidding.

The new prime minister, Nawaz Sharif, a businessman from eastern Punjab, took power later in 1990. Sharif, who tried to get Beg to tone down his anti-American rhetoric, sent one of his ministers, who had a brother who was also a general, to talk to the army chief.

But Beg wanted to talk about Iran, recalled the minister, who requested anonymity: "Beg said: 'Iran is willing, you name the price. Iran is willing to give whatever it takes, $6 billion, $10 billion. We can sell the bomb to Iran at any price and why shouldn't we?'"

Pakistan's civilian government controlled neither the military nor A. Q. Khan and his nuclear program. The anonymous minister added, "We didn't always know what A. Q. Khan was doing when he would make trips and the military always told us not to ask." One of his trips was to North Korea.

During the 1990s, while under U.S. sanctions, Pakistan acquired the North Korean Nodong missile, with a range of 1,000 to 1,300 kilometers, which it copied and reproduced. From China, a longtime ally of Pakistan, it also received M-11 missiles, which can carry a nuclear warhead about 300 kilometers.

But the military's wounds had never healed completely from its 1971 defeat and the 1974 nuclear test by India. It wanted to test its own bomb, which it did, successfully, in May 1998. Both India and Pakistan exploded nuclear devices, and the United States then imposed more sanctions. For Pakistan, already under sanctions, the newest U.S. punishment hardly mattered.

"The military didn't take its orders from us, we took them from the military," said Sharif's minister. But in his second term, Sharif tried to flex his muscles. He was able to force the resignation of the army chief, General Jehangir Karamat. That had never happened before in Pakistan's history.

General Pervez Musharraf was appointed to replace Karamat. At the time, someone who knew both Karamat and Musharraf said of the recently appointed army chief: "He is a commando. He won't be dismissed. If the government tries to fire him, he won't go home and watch television. He'll take over."

And that's what he did in 1999 when Sharif tried to replace him. The world condemned Musharraf. U.S. president Bill Clinton, who had met Sharif several times, condemned the coup and extended the sanctions. But in a piece of diplomatic symbolism, in 2000 Clinton went to Pakistan while on a visit to neighboring

India. The United States didn't approve of Pakistan's military dictator or his support for Afghanistan's Taliban, but Clinton's administration had decided not to completely snub Pakistan while in South Asia.

Clinton's visit was a drama that lasted barely five hours. A decoy aircraft landed before him, and an unsmiling Clinton refused to be televised shaking Musharraf's hand, but he did go on Pakistan's state-run television and lectured Pakistanis on democracy and the foibles of military dictatorships. Pakistanis were chafed and baffled at the apparent hypocrisy. Washington had previously supported Zia's military dictatorship, and less than twenty-four hours after making his televised speech attacking Pakistan's military rule, Clinton was pictured shaking the hand of Syrian dictator Hafiz Assad.

Like Zia, who was embraced by the U.S. after the Soviet invasion of Afghanistan, Musharraf went from U.S. foe to friend after al Qaeda's September 11 attacks on the United States.

U.S. president George W. Bush called Musharraf that night. He told him he had a choice. He was either with the United States or against it. Musharraf promised immediate and unconditional support for the United States and said he could stop Pakistan's support for the Taliban. Overnight, Musharraf went from pariah to valued friend.

Zia and Musharraf had much in common: They were both Indian-born Pakistanis; they had both been rescued from isolation by international events; they had both carried out fraudulent referendums to legitimize their rule; and they had both used the most radical of religious parties, Jamiat-e-Ulema Islam and Jamaat-e-Islami, to sideline mainstream political parties.

In hindsight, it was a mistake to support Zia and his Islamic fervor, which gave rise to extremist militants. The same mistake is being made by supporting Musharraf, whose military is slowly strangling Pakistan's civil society and protecting the religious right.

Under Musharraf's guiding hand, Pakistan's political landscape changed drastically. While espousing moderate Islam, he brought to power regressive, rigidly religious forces in two of Pakistan's four provinces.

Musharraf promised to reform madrassas that incited jihad and intolerance and preached anti-Western hatred, but nothing has been done since he seized power. The massive spending in education promised by Musharraf never materialized; madrassas remain the cheapest and most readily available source of education for Pakistan's poor, who are growing in number; development indicators for Pakistan have dropped; Musharraf's military government has spent less than $500 million on education and health care combined, and more than $3 billion on the military.

Instead of investment in public education, Musharraf convinced the West to spend its money on modernizing madrassas, which would further entrench them. Regardless of how modern a madrassa might be, religious scholars still have to give final approval to its curriculum. Jihad is a tenet of Islam and as such can be justified as being taught in a religious school.

Militant Muslim groups run some of the largest madrassas in Pakistan. Giving them computers and teaching them software programming won't redefine their purpose.

Today, the religious schools in some of the remote border regions harbor fugitive Taliban and espouse the al Qaeda philosophy. They still churn out young recruits imbued with the fervor of jihad.

As Hamid Gul, sitting in his sun-drenched living room, leaning forward, once softly said to me: "Jihad works."

Modernizing madrassas would give more, not less power to religious institutions and churn out more, not fewer graduates to threaten Pakistan and the region's stability.

Musharraf, who has charmed most of Washington with his talk of enlightened Islam, is contemptuous of Pakistan's civil society and its activists.

In 2004, an article appeared in a news magazine written by Asma Jehangir, a human rights lawyer who had battled name-calling radical Islamists to defend minority Christians accused of blasphemy. A small woman, barely five feet tall, Asma had walked into homes of feudal landowners and freed peasants held as slaves on their land. The United Nations made her its special envoy on extrajudicial killings.

The story she wrote was of Muktarai Mai, a young woman whose gang rape had been ordered by a village council as punishment for an affair her young brother was accused of having with an older woman. Asma wrote of the horrific rape, the senselessness of the tribal punishment, the complicity of a silent government—but she also wrote of Muktarai Mai's courage, her refusal to quit, and of a school she opened and the children she taught there.

President Musharraf could not conceal his disdain: He accused Asma of sullying Pakistan's international reputation by writing the story. He made no promise to change the laws, or to attack the system that allowed a woman to be judicially gang-raped. Instead, Musharraf said he wanted to slap the face of Asma for writing the story.

CHAPTER NINE

Ties That Bind

It was a crisp morning in November 2004 when I set off by car for Peshawar.

A riotously colored bus bulging with passengers belched black smoke in our direction as it careened past us, narrowly avoiding taking off the side mirror. Cyclists, hidden beneath woolen shawls, were hunched over their handlebars. The first prayer of the day had just finished, and men with tiny white skull caps perched on their heads emerged from the countless mosques that ran the length of the Grand Trunk Road, built centuries ago to link Kabul to Calcutta.

In the distance, traditional mud homes peeked out from behind the tacky new construction that lined the road. In the fields, men and women squatted, slashing at the wheat with their hand-held scythes, bullock carts pulled handcrafted plows, and it seemed as if time had stood still.

The purpose of the journey was shrouded in secrecy. It had required a series of discreet negotiations that had begun more than a week earlier with a conversation with Karim on his mobile phone. Our conversations were short, intentionally vague and laced with words that were meant to confuse anyone who might be eavesdropping.

The caution was for Karim's protection and for the protection of the man we were to meet. Karim worried that Pakistan's intelligence service was listening in. He was probably right. Once when I ended a telephone call with another contact, my phone had rung and on the other end was an intelligence man, who in his broken English relayed back to me the meat of my conversation, just to demonstrate their capacity for surveillance.

Karim did not travel with me along the Grand Trunk Road. He had disappeared two days earlier, having melted into an underground network where he found Mohammed Hakim, the number three man in Jaish-e-Muslimeen, a group that had broken away from the Taliban.

Hakim was the purpose of the journey. On that November morning in 2004, he was a hunted man. His group was holding three UN workers hostage. The kidnapping had been a daring affair, carried out in the middle of the day in Kabul. The UN vehicle had been stuck in traffic when the gunmen pulled up alongside and hauled the two women and one man from the car.

I sat at a prearranged meeting point at the foot of a bridge waiting for Karim to call. I slouched in the car, my face turned toward the window. My eyes wandered across the street. I saw a couple of policemen shaking down a rickshaw driver. A lot of gesturing occurred before the driver slipped a note into a policeman's hand and drove off. Horns roared as buses and trucks sped past, as daredevil motorcyclists wove in and out of traffic, slipping through spaces that seemed too narrow.

I had begun to think the meeting might not happen, but then the phone rang. It was Karim. He was nearby. Jaish-e-Muslimeen was a murky, almost wholly unknown organization until the kidnapping of the UN workers. The nucleus of the new group were former Taliban, men who were still aligned to the misogynist movement but wanted more violent resistance action than its leader, Mullah Omar, had been giving them. Indeed, there had been almost no public sighting and only rare utterances from Omar since 2001, when he had been driven from Kandahar into the mountainous border region.

There was a massive manhunt in Afghanistan for Jaish-e-Muslimeen members. They had released tapes of the hostages, who had been held together at first but were later separated. When the hostages were first taken, the demands were for the release of Taliban, but later the group focused in on their demand for money. They had threatened several times to kill their captives, had set deadlines, then extended them, then set new ones. It was all rather chaotic.

The hostages would later be freed, but when I met Hakim, it still wasn't known whether they would live or die. Hakim's group had circulated videotapes threatening them with death.

At such a dramatically dangerous time for Jaish-e-Muslimeen, I wondered why Hakim would risk meeting me, and how, despite the cloak-and-dagger approach to our meeting, he was able to move around in Pakistan so freely.

I was mulling this over when someone knocked on my window. It was Karim. He jumped into my car. Hakim was in another car. He followed us. We wound our way deep within the labyrinth of streets that make up Peshawar's ancient city; some of the craggy paths and sidewalks have been around for 2,000 years, and some of the crumbling buildings looked as though they had been as well.

We parked the car in an empty lot, overgrown with tall grass. I was pushed through a nearby gate and up a narrow, steep stone staircase until I reached a small balcony that was encased in a wrought-iron railing twisted in a bizarre design of elongated flowers. The balcony led to a room, carpeted in the traditional Afghan deep red. The house belonged to an Afghan businessman. His name was kept secret. It was obvious by the two large four-wheel-drive vehicles parked inside the compound that he had money.

Pillows were scattered against the wall. Hakim was already there. I looked at him, amazed at how relaxed he seemed. Despite the manhunt in Afghanistan, Hakim seemed to feel safe in Pakistan.

His beard was bushy and unkempt, in keeping with Taliban tradition. He smiled as we began to talk. Although it was during the fasting month of Ramadan, as we started our conversation a young boy, barely ten years old, slipped quietly into the room carrying a tray too big for his small size and poured steaming green tea into my cup. I was the only one drinking during this time of fasting.

Karim hadn't told me much about Hakim. I knew he was from Afghanistan's eastern Nangarhar Province, as Karim was, and that he had fought with the Taliban, although it seemed he had joined the religious movement quite late on. He had been a refugee in Pakistan, like millions of others. I wondered what had brought him to this point. He was somewhere in his late twenties, maybe early thirties. It was difficult to tell, and he himself didn't know exactly how old he was.

Since the Taliban's collapse three years ago, Hakim had been hiding in the mountains of Afghanistan, making regular visits to Pakistan. He eventually tired of the sporadic attacks organized by Mullah Omar and yearned for something bigger, more daring. With a man named Akbar Aga and a group of like-minded Taliban, he branched out, founding Jaish-e-Muslimeen.

The first thing that struck me about Hakim was how willing he was to talk. He was ready to answer any question, but he explained, almost apologetically, that his time was short. He had other appointments later that morning, including one to decide the fate of the hostages. Jaish-e-Muslimeen's leaders were to decide whether to extend the latest deadline for the hostages' release, release them immediately, or kill them.

I was struck by the contrariness of the situation. The hostages were being held in Afghanistan, yet here I was meeting with a senior Jaish-e-Muslimeen man in Pakistan before he was to attend a leadership meeting also here in Pakistan.

According to Hakim, his group had been provoked into kidnapping the UN workers to put an end to the boasting of the United Nations, the Afghan government, and the U.S. administration about the uneventful presidential elections that had been held a month earlier. It had been a spectacular event for Afghans, who had never voted before.

They lined up for hours to mark their ballots. Because the voting was peaceful, the international community declared the resistance too weak to mount an opposition to the polling. For Jaish-e-Muslimeen, that was a challenge.

A crooked smile began to spread across Hakim's face. He stroked his beard, then said:

> They were talking and talking that we couldn't do anything. They were saying we were like women, that we couldn't do anything to harm them. We decided that this wasn't right. We decided to show them that we were not women; they were like women. We captured the hostages in the middle of the day, off the street in Kabul, and no one could stop us or catch us.

Hakim said his group was divided over the fate of the hostages. Hakim wanted them to live, but there were others who wanted to kill them. Hakim said he was even sorry that two of the hostages were women. That wasn't part of the plan. He explained, "If our demands aren't met, maybe we will just take them up into the mountains, and don't worry, we will look after the women and make a nice women's cave."

The conversation was surreal.

Hakim wanted me to know that he wasn't unfeeling. He sympathized with the hostages, and he understood the suffering of their families. But what of the wives and children of the detained Taliban, women whose husbands were taken without warning, without information of their whereabouts or whether they were alive or dead? His answer was: "Our women cry every night; their children cry. We are suffering too. We want everyone to feel our suffering."

He understood that kidnapping the UN workers wasn't gaining him any sympathy: "I know this but we have no choices." Hakim warned of more attacks.

The conversation ended suddenly, even though I had many more questions that I would have liked to ask. Hakim had to leave. But he wanted me to wait upstairs while he left.

I did, but just long enough for him to get out the door—and then I raced down to catch a glimpse of the license plate of his car as he sped through the narrow alleyway. It began with the number 83. The plates had been provided by the ISI, Pakistan's intelligence agency.

That explained why he seemed so relaxed moving around in Pakistan. The plate protected him. In Peshawar, any plate beginning with the number 83 has been provided exclusively by or for the ISI. It immediately connotes status, like a diplomatic plate on an embassy vehicle.

The same day that Hakim and I discussed the hostage taking, General Pervez Musharraf—Pakistan's president and Washington's anti-terrorist ally—was in Afghanistan. He had gone to Afghanistan to congratulate Hamid Karzai, the country's newly elected president.

That evening on television, hours after Hakim and his Jaish-e-Muslimeen had held their council meeting to decide whether to spare or kill the hostages, I watched as Musharraf shook Karzai's hand and promised him Pakistan's support to fight terrorism. It made me contemplate the murkiness of Musharraf's agenda.

On the one hand, Musharraf had sent his soldiers into the violent South Waziristan tribal areas, where nearly 200 were killed trying to flush out suspected terrorists, and on the other hand, his intelligence agency protected men who had kidnapped international UN workers.

For years the Pakistani military had played both sides of the fence: saying one thing but doing another; closing militant training camps in one area and reopening them in another; calling for enlightened moderation while shutting down one terrorist organization and letting it reopen under another name.

The events of September 11, 2001, in the United States did not erase decades of Pakistan military policy that both used jihadis to fight its proxy wars and looked toward Afghanistan for its strategic depth against neighbor India, even during good times between the two countries.

The collapse of the Taliban had left Pakistan dealing with an Afghan government that looked at it with suspicion and to India for friendship, aid, and perhaps even military and intelligence cooperation. Unable to send its own people to spy on India in Afghanistan, Pakistan effortlessly found Afghan recruits among its former Taliban allies and even in the al Qaeda ranks.

Jihadis nurtured and spawned decades before by the Pakistan military and its intelligence were recruited and trained in camps tucked away in Pakistan's remote regions. There was one in Bajour Agency in the Northwest Frontier Province and in Khorazon in Baluchistan Province, not so many kilometers from where Musharraf's military was waging its U.S.-backed battles against suspected terrorists, a war seen by local tribesmen as being more about cowing them than rounding up foreign fighters.

In December 2002, more than one year after Pakistan promised its unconditional support for the United States and its war on terrorism, I saw a video of a graduation ceremony held in Pakistan's Baluchistan Province for graduates of a training camp. Several men in black turbans sat on a makeshift stage, while at the microphone a firebrand hurled abuses at the United States, inspiring young graduates to battle the infidel.

The training courses lasted two weeks. Some trainees among them had signed up to be suicide bombers; others would be logistics men. Men were taught to detonate bombs by remote control, as well as how to ram an explosive-laden vehicle into a target. Arab instructors provided the motivation. They nurtured in their recruits the desire to die for their cause in pursuit of heavenly rewards. Among the instructors were former Pakistani intelligence and military men.

Suicide bombers were encouraged to travel in pairs, taking

inspiration from each other. A selection of possible targets was given to the suicide bombers, who would spend a week or more running through the possibilities before settling on the best target. The families of suicide bombers were promised $50,000 in compensation.

Najibullah, a young man barely twenty-three years old when I spoke to him in 2003, had undergone training. Above all, he wanted me to understand that he wasn't afraid to die. He spoke rapidly. His venom was for the United States. "I went there [training camp] to learn to kill the foreign troops in Afghanistan. We will drive them out because they are destroying our country." Nearly two years after the September 11, 2001, attacks, Najibullah told me that at his camp there were Pakistanis, Afghans, Southeast Asians, and Arabs, all training to kill or sacrifice themselves to the cause.

The camps were small and easily moved, and occasionally it had been necessary to decamp when a U.S. helicopter got too close or villagers had asked them to leave.

As we spoke, Najibullah carefully pulled from an inside pocket a small piece of frayed wood called a *maswak*, the ancient form of a toothbrush ripped from a tree and used by Islam's prophet Mohammed.

Najibullah held it with a great deal more reverence than a traditional toothbrush deserved, but that was because of who had owned it before him.

"This was from Osama," he said. Bin Laden hadn't personally given it to Najibullah, but a friend had received it from the al Qaeda boss and had given it to Najibullah. His friend was dead, killed in a suicide attack.

Najibullah was unafraid: "No one can stop us."

The Pakistani military and its intelligence runs like a thread through the jihadi fabric. It gave birth to jihadi groups and helped fuse the groups and their leaders into a global network. That is why, in each set of the eleven-volume *Encyclopedia of Jihad,* each volume begins with the same four pages of tributes: to bin Laden; to Abdullah Azam, bin Laden's mentor, who was killed in a suicide bombing in Pakistan in the early 1980s; to the Islamic leaders of Afghanistan; and to Pakistan.

Pakistan's military and its ISI opened the door to militant Muslims during the Afghan war against the Soviets. Their fervor was harnessed to defeat the former Soviet Union, referred to then as the home of godless infidels.

The Middle Eastern fighters who answered the call to jihad in the 1980s had a vision of their own, the creation of a pan-Islamic union that would spread their extreme interpretation of Islam throughout the Muslim world. They found like-minded men among the Afghan fighters, men who shared their dream of an Islamic world united within one border.

The United States returned some like Sayyaf and Burhanuddin Rabbani to positions of influence in Afghanistan following the collapse of the Taliban and made allies of the Pakistan military, which had spawned some of the fiercest jihadis and embraced some of the most conservative of Pakistan's religious groups, such as Jamaat-e-Islami, whose members have ties with al Qaeda men that span decades. These religious conservatives fought in battle in Afghanistan. They plotted to send fighters to conflicts in Chechnya and Bosnia and on Pakistan's eastern front in Kashmir.

The links between the ISI, the Taliban, the mujahedeen in Kabul today, and Arab al Qaeda were forged in battle from Bosnia to Kashmir as well as Afghanistan and have not been broken. Since 9/11, most of the top al Qaeda suspects who have been arrested in Pakistan have been found in houses belonging to Jamaat-e-Islami men and women.

They include the likes of Abu Zubayda, the al Qaeda money-man and financier of the September 11 attacks. Zubayda had set up at least five companies through which al Qaeda moved its money around the world, financed the training of the suicide pilots who executed the airborne assaults that launched the U.S. war on terror. Months before he was arrested, I had met men who knew Abu Zubayda, who knew where he was. It wasn't until

U.S. intelligence kicked in, tracked him down, and forced his arrest that he was picked up in Faisalabad in Pakistan in a dwelling belonging to a Jamaat-e-Islami member.

Exactly one year after the 9/11 attacks, another of the most-wanted al Qaeda men, Ramzi Bin Al Shahib, was arrested after a shootout in Karachi, in the home of a Jamaat-e-Islami follower. One of Bin Al Shahib's comrades killed in the shootout wrote "Death to America" in blood on the wall before he died.

One of the biggest arrests in the war against terrorists was Khalid Sheikh Mohammed, said to have helped mastermind the September 11 attacks. In March 2003, he was taken as he slept in the home of a Jamaat-e-Islami member.

Months before Khalid's capture, I had been in Peshawar at the school where he had once lectured. I spoke to men who knew him, who said he had been in Peshawar just weeks before I got there. What struck me was how much information was available on his whereabouts.

A former ISI man told me that most of these men, who had been jihadis from the Afghan war, were told soon after September 11, 2001, that Pakistan would not come looking for them, but if they were discovered by U.S. intelligence, they would be arrested. The warning was intended to make them discreet.

Jamaat-e-Islami adherents had dominated Pakistan's secret service since the 1980s. They had forged the ties with the militant Muslims, distributed money and weapons, and were close to men like Khalid Sheikh Mohammed, Gulbuddin Hekmatyar, and Abdul Rasul Sayyaf.

But despite the glaring connection between Jamaat-e-Islami and al Qaeda operatives, the religious party was not investigated in Pakistan. There were reasons: Jamaat-e-Islami adherents dominated the ranks of the Pakistan military.

As early as 1970, Jamaat-e-Islami began to infiltrate the military and bureaucracy, where its members soon became entrenched.

Jamaat-e-Islami's ideology is regressive and rigid. It supports segregating women, imposing purdah, and imposing strict Islamic law based on literal interpretations of the Quran. It has been the most outspoken opponent of changing regressive Islamic laws such as the Hadood Ordinance and has fought against outlawing honor killings and granting rights to women. It supports changing the financial structure to an Islamic system, which would do away with interest payments, and it has publicly supported Pakistan's nuclear program and its sharing of its nuclear technology with other Islamic countries.

Jihad is at the core of Jamaat-e-Islami, whose militant wing, Hezb-ul Mujahedeen, has trained and sent men to fight in Bosnia, Chechnya, and Kashmir, and has encouraged China's Uighurs to revolt. According to Javed Nasir, a former ISI chief and a rigid Islamist himself, the organization fomented Islamic revolt in northeastern China. He said he warned Jamaat-e-Islami about stirring up the sentiment of China's Uighurs because it would boomerang and hurt the Uighurs. Nasir also said Jamaat-e-Islami smuggled fighters through Afghanistan to Chechnya, and into Bosnia. Saudi Arabia also sent money to Jamaat-e-Islami under the guise of educational funding.

Jamaat-e-Islami's structure is robust, organized, and frightening. The organization breaks down into subgroups designed to target specific groups: students, teachers, trade unionists, businessmen, and farmers. Its strategy is patient and pragmatic, and it devotes itself to slow, methodical infiltration. Jamaat-e-Islami aims to set up an Islamic state in Pakistan by using a strategy of fomenting Islamic revolt from within.

The structure of the organization is like none other in Pakistan. It operates in cells. The largest, and the underpinning of the organization, is the Shabab-e-Milli cell, with a membership of about 85,000 young men, the agitators who can be mobilized for demonstrations.

In 2004 and early 2005, Jamaat-e-Islami did not call these agitators onto the street to protest Musharraf's refusal to give up either the job of president or army chief because it did not want a confrontation with the military, despite its rhetoric. Any denunciations of the military's role in Pakistan's government were hollow. They were intended to give Jamaat-e-Islami the veneer of being democratic and to give the military a religious opponent against which they could suggest their secularism.

But it was smoke and mirrors.

Jamaat-e-Islami has established nearly 1,300 religious schools, none of which are regulated by the government. It has created the Islamic Medical Association, the National Labor Federation, and the Pakistan Business Forum. It has a powerful students' organization called Islami Jamiat-e-Tulaba, which has infiltrated universities, often intimidating more secular student organizations. It even has a students' union among madrassas, which is powerful and unchallenged.

Jamaat-e-Islami's Al Khidmat Foundation, a social welfare organization registered in Pakistan, spent nearly 43 million rupees in a single year, slightly less than $1 million. It operates openly in other countries.

Jamaat-e-Islami has a special Afghan Fund, while also being closely linked to Afghan insurgents and wanted terrorists such as Gulbuddin Hekmatyar. It has a Chechnya Fund, a Central Asia Fund, and a Bangladesh Affectees' Fund, all of which operate without any controls by the government. They are funds that can be used to transfer money, to recruit, to indoctrinate.

Yet there has been no attempt to freeze or control the assets of Jamaat-e-Islami, despite its members' having harbored top al Qaeda men.

Its militant wing, Hezb-ul Mujahedeen, was one of the first jihadi organizations to be recruited by Pakistan to wage its proxy war against India in Indian-ruled Kashmir. After 1989, the jihadi network was burgeoning and the battlefields multiplying. Pakistan's military and ISI spawned some of the most dangerous of jihadi groups. Among them are Harakat-ul Mujahedeen, Jaish-e-Mohammed, Lashkar-e Tayyaba, Harakat-ul Jihad-e-Islami, Sipah-e-Sahabah Pakistan, and Lashkar-e-Janghvi—just so many strange-sounding names to the English ear. But these groups bound together dangerous men who were united in their desire for a rigid form of Islamic rule that had no borders and was united by a greater Islamic identity.

Tracing the jihadi groups is like following a family tree: One group begets another, begets another, and on down the line.

During the Taliban's rule, Mullah Khaksar, the Taliban's former deputy interior minister, told me that the police couldn't touch the foreign fighters in Afghanistan: "They were all protected by the Taliban leadership, but their money and instructions came directly from Pakistan's ISI."

Harakat-ul Mujahedeen leaders Fazlur Rahman Khalil, Maulana Masood Alvi, and Saifullah Shaukat bonded with Jalaluddin Haqqani, who is a wanted terrorist today, and with Maulvi Younis Khalis, who is now considered a U.S. ally. Both men still have strong ties to Middle Eastern fighters and neither man has abandoned them.

Bin Laden and Aymen al-Zawahri fought alongside Abdul Rasul Sayyaf, who is a U.S. ally today. Yet his refugee camp in Pakistan had been a magnet for militant Muslims from every country, and they in turn forged strong ties with their Pakistani and Afghan militant hosts.

The jihadi groups created by Pakistan were like a virus whose spores scattered and mutated. Harakat-ul Islam begat Harakat-ul Mujahedeen, and Harakat-ul Mujahedeen begat Jaish-e-Mohammed.

In 1989, Harakat-ul Mujahedeen was one of the first jihadi groups to relocate its jihad from Afghanistan to Kashmir, armed, outfitted, and trained by Pakistan's ISI.

The uprising in Indian Kashmir had some homegrown roots in a population disgruntled by a 1989 election result. India was accused of rigging that election. The secessionist group that spearheaded the uprising was a pro-independence one with secular roots called the Jammu-Kashmir Liberation Front. But like the Taliban in Afghanistan, the Pakistan military and its ISI hijacked the secessionist uprising and handed it over to jihadis, who used religion as their rallying cry.

In the early 1990s, when the United States began to express concern about Pakistani militants in Indian Kashmir and threatened to declare Pakistan a terrorist state because of its support for militants, the military relocated its camps to Afghanistan, where the mujahedeen government ruled and training camps already existed, some dating back to the 1980s Soviet war.

When the pressure subsided, the military returned some of its camps to Pakistani-controlled Kashmir.

In 1993, a new mutation, Harakat-ul Ansar, appeared, again operating in Kashmir. It kidnapped and killed a group of British and American backpackers in 1995. Western intelligence agencies suspected Harakat-ul Ansar was the mastermind, and so Pakistan was forced to ban the organization, which it did. But almost immediately it reinvented it in another form, under the banners of Harakat-ul Mujahedeen and Harakat-ul Jihad.

Harakat-ul Mujahedeen cells burgeoned within the military itself, and in the mid-1990s, jihadis within the military were powerful enough to flex their muscles openly. It was Harakat-ul Mujahedeen military men who staged the coup to oust Benazir Bhutto from power. The jihadis had become major generals.

Qari Saifullah, a Harakat-ul Mujahedeen leader who helped mastermind the coup, slipped across the border into Afghanistan. In September 2004, he was arrested in Dubai and accused of being involved in the failed attempts to kill Pakistan's president, Pervez Musharraf.

Musharraf has been walking a very fine line since the September 11, 2001, attacks. Despite its alliance with the United States in the war on terror, Pakistan's military has not abandoned its use of jihadis, primarily as a proxy force against India.

Musharraf's march forward is dictated by his past. While personally a man of moderate Muslim beliefs, he is also a military hawk who was one of the masterminds of an incursion into Indian-ruled Kashmir in 1999. Musharraf ordered army regulars and jihadis into Kargil in Kashmir, took over some Indian territory, and brought the Asian subcontinent dangerously close to all-out war.

Musharraf harbored a deep resentment toward Pakistan's civilian prime minister at the time for seeking to broker a peace deal with India. The Kargil invasion was a debacle.

Musharraf's military training as a commando also defines his style, which men who know him say reveals a propensity to act impetuously.

Musharraf was army chief in 1998 when the military's jihadi creation, Harakat-ul Mujahedeen, operated two training camps in Afghanistan's eastern Paktia Province. The camps were called Khalid bin Walid and Muawyia.

Those were the two camps that U.S. Tomahawk cruise missiles hit in August 1998, aimed supposedly at bin Laden, who was not there. Twenty Pakistani militants, all of them members of Pakistan's Harakat-ul Mujahedeen, were killed in the strikes.

Within days of the attacks in Paktia Province, Mullah Omar announced bin Laden had disappeared, saying that perhaps he had left the country, but in any case, his whereabouts were no longer known. Mullah Omar wouldn't be dragged into speculation about where bin Laden might be.

But if he was not in Afghanistan, then where? The Pakistan army gave him sanctuary to ease U.S. pressure on the Taliban.

A Taliban who had traveled in the convoy that brought bin Laden to Pakistan told me that the al Qaeda chief was hidden at Chirat, a commando training base in northwest Pakistan where Musharraf had trained as a young army officer.

Bin Laden arrived at Chirat in a convoy of four-wheel-drive vehicles. The former Taliban told me that there must have been around twenty vehicles there. Bin Laden brought several of his Arab bodyguards and some senior Taliban leaders with him. They stayed in Chirat for several weeks. The former Taliban said, "The whole idea at the time was to confuse the Americans. Mullah Omar couldn't order him out of the country, but he needed to do something about the pressure from the United States."

Mullah Omar needed some breathing space and Pakistan provided it. Bin Laden had simply disappeared, and at the time no one seemed to know where he was—except the Pakistani military.

That may still be true today.

Four Years Later

Afghanistan's tragedy is that to the world's powers, it has never really mattered—or has not mattered for long. It has never been valued for itself. In the chronology of its history, Afghanistan has repeatedly played the role of pawn in a larger power game: to the imperial British, it was a buffer against the imperial Russians; to India, a sphere of influence from which to irritate Pakistan; to the United States during the Soviet war, a proxy battlefield on which to injure the Soviet Union; to Pakistan, a place of experimental jihadism; and to the United States at the beginning of the twenty-first century, an appropriately otherworldly stage for military-political theater. No country has acted out of long-term concern for the Afghan people. Afghanistan—a "failed state"—points to a long list of distinguished power brokers who participated in its failure. With each dismal repetition, the cycle of history further condemned Afghanistan to victimhood and ensured that the mistakes of the past reverberate far into the future.

One of the greatest mistakes the United States made in both Afghanistan and Pakistan was to believe that "the enemy of my enemy is my friend." That philosophy has had consequences that might be thought hilarious, were they not so catastrophic.

This reasoning led the United States to embrace those who

also held the Taliban as their mortal enemy, despite the fact that such men as Abdul Rasul Sayyaf counted both bin Laden and al-Zawahri among his friends, and Rashid Dostum was a friend of Gulbuddin Hekmatyar. For the United States to expect Sayyaf's and Dostum's militiamen to hunt down bin Laden and his al Qaeda network was a woefully negligent misreading of the political reality in Afghanistan.

In the end, a cruel joke has been played on Afghans. They believed the rhetoric of the West when it promised not to repeat the mistakes of the past and abandon Afghanistan, as it had after the Soviet Union withdrew in 1989 and the Communist regime collapsed in 1992.

But that's exactly what has happened. Apart from Kabul, Afghanistan today looks remarkably like the Afghanistan of 1992. Once again, it has been carved up by and relinquished to the Afghan warlords, who have stepped in to fill the vacuum left by a United States not prepared to provide the soldiers and the funding needed to rebuild over the long term. Afghanistan, as before, is newly fractured and unstable.

The international community hasn't done much better, offering a mere $5 billion over five years, considerably less than the amount given to Kosovo after the war there. Afghans have received $50 per capita; Kosovars, $500 per capita, ten times as much.

It is four years later, and Afghans feel cheated. They have a constitution and a president. But they don't have security, justice, or rule of law. Outside the major cities, where few foreigners venture these days because of the robberies and kidnappings, Afghans are disillusioned, not sure who can be trusted. The West? The rigidly religious Taliban? Neither?

In the last four years, a façade has been created. On the surface, Afghanistan appears to be forging toward democracy and freedom. But beneath that façade are men and militias that harbor a thinly disguised contempt for the West and are knee-deep in the drug trade. They have the patience to wait until an overstretched West pulls out the few soldiers it has stationed there.

Four years later, and Afghanistan still presents the same dangers today that it did before September 11, 2001. One person's story—that of Abu Jandal—made this particularly clear to me.

In a previous life, Abu Jandal was a cloth seller in Morocco. But now he has decided to become a suicide bomber. When I met him, his black beard was long and frizzy, the curls tight and unkempt. His skin was deep olive, his build slight. On his head he wore a small white cap.

Abu Jandal came to Pakistan in 1989, just as the last Soviet soldiers were leaving Afghanistan, retreating after a ten-year occupation. Like thousands of Arab militants before him, he had come to fight communism.

Abu Jandal's childhood offered no clues to his militant future. There was no cataclysmic event that turned him toward militancy, no hatred or anger rooted in one event. He did, however, receive an early introduction to jihad. After he completed the fifth grade, his father sent him to a tutor, an Islamic cleric who taught him his rigid version of the Quran and his interpretations of the teachings of Islam's prophet Mohammed. Abu Jandal remembered, "It was then that I became religious and I thought about the lives of Muslims everywhere and of my religious duty." He was tutored throughout his remaining school years, and as an adult, he said, "I dreamed of becoming a mujahed." And with that dream he went to Afghanistan.

Abu Jandal was raised in a religious home in Morocco. He refused to name his village, afraid it would endanger the family he had left behind, his parents and two brothers. His family was not the poorest, he said. They had a good business, selling clothes and some carpets. They had not encouraged him to go to Afghanistan and fight, but they didn't try to stop him when he came home one day and announced his plans:

> When I came here, I told my mother and father that I was going in the way of Allah. They understood. They didn't cry. Of course my mother should miss me. Every mother remembers her son and every son remembers his mother. We are hu-

man. We are not animals. But I am here now and I cannot talk to them. I cannot call them. My government is against me, and if I try to contact them or if the government comes to know I tried, they will have problems. They have given me in the way of Allah.

He paid his own fare to Pakistan. He came with two friends. His voice was soft and low as he continued his story:

I told my family I should fight in the way of Allah. In Islam it is said that when I die, if I die a martyr, I can take seventy people from the hill [the earth] to heaven. Every martyr can do this. And so when I die, I can take more of my family with me, so it is good for my family as well. But I know that if I die, I will go right to heaven. Allah has promised to me that "I will give you life if you are martyred. If you are martyred there will be no punishment on Judgment Day." For a suicide bomber this world is nothing. There is no sadness. There is a joy, happiness. The life in heaven is very big and will continue for thousands of years. This is what I want.

I met Abu Jandal because I wanted to know what made someone ready to die. Did they hate deeply? Was it about our way of life, or was it more about their own life and the impotency they felt to change it?

Historically, neither Afghans nor Pakistanis have embraced suicide bombings as a means to their end. But Abu Jandal said that was no longer true, that today Pakistani and Afghan recruits are stepping forward to train as suicide bombers: "Islam is not especially for Arabs. Pakistanis and Afghans now are also ready to be martyred to be suicide bombers. More people are getting training in suicide bombings, more people are ready to die because Muslims are under attack in the world." Al Qaeda, he said, receives plenty of volunteers.

Our conversation took place two months before the 2004

U.S. presidential election. Abu Jandal was rooting for President George W. Bush: "We pray to Allah that once again Bush wins the election. Bush is a stupid guy. For us, Bush has been the one who has given us too many people to fight [is perceived as bullying Muslims and Muslim countries]. Because of him we will fight more and more. Today every Muslim wants revenge. People should know that he is the one that has crushed America, but America doesn't know that."

As a knowledgeable al Qaeda member, Abu Jandal knew precise details about suicide bombings in Kabul; he personally knew some of the dead bombers. He was introduced to me by an Arabic-speaking Afghan, a man I knew had fought alongside Arab militants during the 1980s war in Afghanistan. Abu Jandal understood the routine of the successful suicide bomber:

> Anyone who gets training to carry out a suicide attack is given a small map that says such and such places are important, and you should target them whenever you get an opportunity. Sometimes a suicide bomber spends one day, one week in a place until he can attack. Haza Somali, who was a Hafiz-e-Quran person [student of the Quran] was in Paktia's Shigin area, and he attacked a motorcade and killed six people, including himself. Another friend of mine, Abdur Rahman from Algeria, died last year in Kabul. He had been living for a long time in Kabul. He had maps of important places. Near Pul-e-Charkhi, he attacked the ISAF [international peacekeeping] forces and killed two of them and himself. He was my close friend. We had lived together in Jalalabad and Khost and Kandahar.

Abu Jandal isn't a significant cog in the al Qaeda organization, just a foot soldier who wants to die by blowing up himself and his perceived enemies. He gained experience fighting with several mujahedeen leaders during the Soviet invasion. He fought with Gulbuddin Hekmatyar, and with Sayyaf.

Abu Jandal was in Afghanistan when the mujahedeen took power in 1992. After that, he traveled freely between Pakistan and Afghanistan. He spent most of his time either in Paktia Province or in Jalalabad, in eastern Nangarhar Province. He said that under the mujahedeen government, terrorist training camps flourished: "There were many camps in the mujahedeen time. Some of the camps were run by Arabs and some by Punjabis and some by Afghans. The mujahedeen came from different countries and some would go back to fight against their governments. There were no problems for us in the camps before the Taliban." But during the Taliban rule, he said, the coordination improved: "Then more brothers were able to operate together. There was a Chechen faction, [and one for] Somalia and [the] Chinese, and [for] people from different other countries. They were able to operate together without any problems."

Abu Jandal hopes that a pure Islamic state will be established in Morocco: "In my country there is great immorality. Adultery and drinking is common. There is no difference today between my country and Bush's country."

He worries that the struggle for an Islamic Morocco will be difficult. The government there has made it difficult for al Qaeda to establish large-scale training camps, although local recruits manage to operate small cells, as they do in other countries in the Middle East, Europe, and the United States. Bin Laden and senior al Qaeda men both in Afghanistan and Pakistan have devised strategies and have sent them to local recruits to execute. Abu Jandal commented:

It's easier for us in Afghanistan. We know where to go. We know the country, the mountains, where to hide. It is not difficult for us to move around in Afghanistan. In Pakistan we have friends, too, but it does not have the protection we get in the mountains.

Jihad is not finished. Who said jihad is finished? It will last until the Day of Judgment. You should know that it is going on in Somalia, in Palestine, in the Philippines, in Kashmir, against America.

The mother of the problem is America in the world. They started the struggle and the war against al Qaeda. America announced if anyone kills Osama he would be rich. Day by day America helps Israel. They give weapons to the Israelis to use against the Arabs, and how many innocent Arabs die. Two things you should know. America is the enemy of humankind and also is especially the enemy of Muslims.

Our conversation came to an end outside a grand white mosque in Peshawar. We stopped the car we had been driving around in. I waited for Abu Jandal to get out, but he didn't move, making me wonder whether he was nervous, afraid of who might be out there on the street. Might he be in danger? Was there a police officer nearby he was worried about?

I searched the faces of the people on the sidewalk outside the mosque: An old man with a white turban wrapped carelessly around his head was selling some kind of nuts scattered on a woven straw plate, some children played nearby, and dozens of men ambled past, showing no interest in us. There was nothing alarming.

Then, turning back to Abu Jandal, I saw that in his lap his hands cradled a grenade. What struck me first, even before the thought of what he might do with it, was the bright gold of the pin. I have seen many grenades, but always old ones, and never have they been shoved in my face with the pin still gleaming.

The grenade had been pulled out of a white terry cloth pouch, which looked custom-made.

"You see this grenade? It is with me always. If anyone tries to capture me, I will kill them and myself."

He slipped the grenade back in the pouch and left without another word.

As he walked away, I realized that armies could not win this war on terror, because their enemy is a guerrilla fighter. And the bigger the army, the more vulnerable the soft targets—the schools, the roadside checkpoints, the innocent workers. Nor would the war be won by warlords who had been returned to power under the cloak of democracy and freedom, nor by the military dictators of Pakistan, nor by the use of force or threat of force.

The West has to take a critical look at itself and examine the apparent double standards at work that allow it to attack Iraq for possessing weapons of mass destruction but not North Korea, whose leader shares Saddam Hussein's megalomaniacal qualities; that permit it to rail against Iran about nuclear weapons but be silent about Israel's arsenal; that allow it to only selectively demand enforcement of UN resolutions. The West has to own up to the mistakes it has made: such as with Abu Ghraib and the torture in Afghan prisons; in the errant attacks on civilians; in its disregard for the basic precept of a civilized legal system, which maintains that an accused person is innocent until proven guilty.

The nature of the torture at Abu Ghraib reflected the West's perception of Muslims, hence the women soldiers who seemed to take such delight in the outrages and the especially humiliating use of dogs, considered abhorrent to Muslims, and the practice of making prisoners perform demeaning sexual acts.

The torture was based on a phobic perception of Islam. Had Saddam Hussein's soldiers carried out these abuses on American soldiers, the outrage would have been global and the retribution violent. But because it was American and British soldiers who committed the torture, the blame was attached only to a few, to soldiers we were told were an aberration.

I watched Abu Jandal enter the mosque. His final words to me were these:

> It is not possible to make peace when all the attacks are against Muslims. Tell me why is the USA against Pakistan having nuclear weapons, when Israel and India can have these weapons and no one is saying anything against them? Why, when a Muslim country does something, everyone is

ready to attack? Why, when a non-Muslim country does the same thing, no one attacks? I strongly believe that the CIA has launched wars throughout the world with just one agenda in mind and that is to crush Muslims. But I say openly I will fight against the United States and its allies.

ACKNOWLEDGMENTS

This book is the culmination of eighteen years covering Afghanistan and Pakistan as a reporter. I have many people to thank for their help, but the entire list would be another book.

My AP colleagues in both Afghanistan and Pakistan have helped me uncover the secrets of the two countries. Amir Shah, in Afghanistan, has been both friend and colleague; his gentle heart and amazing resilience have carried me through wars, the repressive Taliban regime, and the mujahedeen's violent rule. He has never refused to go anywhere, meet anyone, take any risks. He is a true hero.

In Pakistan, my colleague Zaman Kazmi was selfless with his time, digging through the AP archives for me, organizing and printing my manuscript.

There are countless others: my Taliban friend Mullah Mohammed Khaksar, who was brave enough to talk to me when the Taliban ruled, who cared so deeply for his country that he joined the Taliban and later left them; the AP, for giving me the support and leave of absence I needed to write the book; Carole Hyatt, who helped me take the first steps that led to this book; Janullah Hashinzada, who dreams of a thriving Afghanistan; and countless Afghans and Pakistanis, whose generosity reminds me daily why I feel so fortunate to have made my home here.

When I began my journey to this part of the world in 1986, it was in the company of my friend Joe Gaal, a man of gentle, kind, and soul-soothing spirit. He died not long after the last Soviet soldier left Afghanistan in 1989, burned out from photographing the brutal killing perpetrated by the Communist regime of that time in an exceptional body of work. He continues to live in my heart.

I thank my friends Françoise Chipaux, whose encouragement kept me focused and whose generosity of spirit and patience with my endless questions contributed to the book's completion; Chris Fisher, whose perseverance and selflessness inspired me and whose edit of my manuscript gave me the courage to submit it; and Ruth Murray and Mike Levin, a source of support for more than two decades. Thanks to my two oldest friends, Brenda Rentelis and Irene Young.

I am grateful to other friends as well: Suzy Goldenberg, whose reporting for the *Guardian* on the Israel, Palestine, and Iraq war was some of the finest and the bravest, who helped me with her advice, encouragement, and humor; and Paula Newberg, whose brilliance shows in every word she writes, who was kind and generous with her advice, wisdom, and experience.

Thanks are also due to these friends: Heidi and Timmi Amin, whose love and support never failed; Diane Handal, who never doubted me and was always a source of encouragement; Salima Hashmi, who inspired me with her inexhaustible spirit and love; Gulshan and Iftikar Rashid, for their selfless friendship and love; Mahmood Durrani, who cares deeply for his country and its progress; Zahid Hussain, who gave so generously of his knowledge; Mary Anne Weaver, who was unstinting in her help and encouragement; and Ahmed Rashid, who was kind enough to say I should get a Pulitzer before anyone was even paying attention to Afghanistan.

A special thank you to Sister Catherine Fairbairn, who has inspired generations with her compassion and me when I needed it most. She said it best when she said: "We are so ignorant of the history, culture, religion, and people of the Muslim nations. We will never have peace until there is an openness to learn about and appreciate Eastern civilizations."

And without my family—my husband, Naeem Pasha, and my stepdaughter, Kyla Pria Pasha—this book would never have happened. Kyla taught me to trust myself, inspiring me with her heart and the depth of her soul. I am forever grateful to Pasha for letting me share in his daughter's life, for inspiring me with his dreams, for his strength when I needed it most and his wisdom, which has guided me through our years together. He taught me the richness of Pakistan's history and shared with me his love for his culture, music, and art.

I am grateful to my niece Maureen Fergus, a talented writer, who gave generously of herself, encouraging and supporting me.

I give thanks to my mother, who loved me unconditionally and suffered silently through my difficult times; to my sister and best friend, Patricia Ann, who is selfless to me and to anyone in need; and to my brothers, Ed, Robert, and Terry, whom I always looked up to and who were a constant source of encouragement and support. They were my strength.

I am grateful to my publisher, Peter Osnos, for wanting the untold stories to be told, for wanting to get the truth out even when it is unpopular, and for being one of the few heroes left in the business; to my editor, Clive Priddle, whose guiding hand was strong, solid, and unfailingly insightful; to my agent, Lynn Nesbit; to David Remnick, *The New Yorker* editor, for accepting my story proposal and fulfilling my dream of writing for *The New Yorker;* to Sharon Delano, who encouraged me and was my editor on my *New Yorker* piece; to Susanna Margolis, who assisted me in my proposal; and to the countless people who have opened their hearts to me.

INDEX

Abbas, Mullah Mohammed, 106
Abdullah, Abdullah, 2
Abu Ghraib, 172
Abu Sayyaf, 142
Adam, Farooq, 131–134
    pardon of, 138
Afghan Fund, 160
Afghan Interior Ministry, 11–12
Afghanistan
    bombing of, 97–98
    foreign fighters in, 75–76
    leadership in, 124
    Musharraf in, 154
    Pakistan and, 92
    removal of Westerners from, 92
    sanctions on, 77
    Soviet invasion of, 139
Aga, Akbar, 152
Aga, Sher, 97
Aga, Tayyab, 42
Ahmed, Mahmood, 92–93
    Haqqani and, 94
    Omar and, 93–94
Ahmedis, 136
Ahmedzai, Shahpur, 52
Al Jazeera, 92
    bombing of, 106
Al Khidmat Foundation, 160
Alcohol, 4
    in Pakistan, 138
Ali, Hazrat, 115, 116
Alvi, Maulana Masood, 161
Amanullah, Ex-King of Afghanistan
    (Wild), 46
Amanullah, King of Afghanistan, 46
Amir-ul Momineen, 42, 44–45
Ariana Airlines, 80

Assad, Hazif, 146
Associated Press
    theft from, 28
    Zaheeruddin and, 3
Attock Conspiracy, 134
Azam, Abdullah, 87, 141
    Encyclopedia of Jihad and, 157

Babaar, Nasrullah, 40
Bagram prison, 121–122
Bajour Agency, 155
Bamiyan, 77–78
    Shah, Amir, in, 80–81
Banking, in Pakistan, 141–142
BBC, 89, 105
Beg, Mirza Aslam, 143, 144
Beg, Rehmat, 125
Berlin Wall, 8
Bhutto, Benazir, 142–143
Bhutto, Zulfikar Ali, 133–134
    Haq, Zia-ul, and, 136
    Islam and, 135, 138
    on nuclear weapons, 135
    overthrow of, 138
Bibi, Aysha, 116
Bibi, Rabia, 47–48
Bin Al Shahib, Ramzi, 158
Bin Laden, Osama, 5
    Azam and, 141
    in Bamiyan, 77–78
    CIA and, 62–63
    disappearance of, 164
    elusiveness of, 95
    Encyclopedia of Jihad and, 156–157
    financing by, 77
    Hekmatyar and, 17
    introduction of, 35

Bin Laden, Osama *(cont.)*
    in Kandahar, 76
    Omar and, 31–32, 93
    protection of, 92–93
    recruitment by, 73
    reward for, 65
    Sayyaf and, 161
    strength of, 62
    support for, 32
    Taliban and, 163
    terrorism and, 85
    United States attack on, 75
Booby-traps, 16
Bosnia, 38–39
Britain
    bombing by, 107
    Pakistan and, 127–129
Buddhism, 78–79
Burjan, Mullah, 48–49
Bush, George W., 14
    Musharraf and, 146
    reelection of, 169

Casey, Bill, 140
Cassell, Nancy, 86
Central Bank, 100
Central Treaty Organization
        (CENTO), 131
    Soviet Union and, 132
    United States and, 132
Charasyab, 12
Chechnya, 39
China, 39
    Beg, Mirza Aslam, and, 144
    nuclear weapons and, 145
    Uighurs of, 159
Chirat, 163–164
CIA
    bin Laden and, 62–63
    ISI and, 140
    Khaksar and, 62–65
    Taliban and, 32
Clarke, Richard C., 31
Clinton, Bill, 145–146
Cloak of the Prophet, 45–46
CNN, 90
Communism, downfall of, 8
Computers, 86

Corruption, 27–29
Curry, Dayna, 84, 107–108

Dadullah, Mullah, 43–44
Dah Rawood, 117
Dasht-e-Barchi, 13
Donahue, David, 91
Dostum, Abdul Rashid, 10
    Hekmatyar and, 14, 16–17
    rape and, 68
    Taliban and, 67–68
    United States and, 166
Drugs. *See also* Heroin; Opium
    Sherzai and, 29
    Taliban and, 55

Education
    Jamaat-e-Islami and, 160
    in Pakistan, 147
    women and, 49
Eid, 116
Eid Gah Mosque, 45
Encyclopedia of Jihad, 87, 156–157

F–86 Saber jets, 131
Fahim, Mohammed, 52, 123
Farid, Babar, 33–34
Faruqi, Mohammed, 111–112
Freedom fighters, 4

Gandhi, Mahatma, 128
Gardez, 109, 115
Gazetteer, 79
Ghadaffi, Muammar, 136
Ghafoor, Maulvi Abdul, 117
Ghous, Mullah, 71
Gorbachev, Mikhail, 142–143
    Red Army and, 5
Guantanamo, 120–121
Gul, Hamid, 138, 143
Gul, Sher, 60

Hadiths, 93
Hadood Ordinance, 141
    Jamaat-e-Islami and, 159
Hajj, 136
Hakim, Mohammed, 151–154
Haq, Abdul, 58

Haq, Zia-ul, 136–137
  coup of, 138–139
  death of, 142
  Reagan and, 141
  United States and, 139
Haqqani, Jalaluddin, 94, 161
Harakat-e-Islami, 77
Harakat-ul Ansar, 162
Harakat-ul Islam, 161
Harakat-ul Jihad, 162
Harakat-ul Mujahedeen, 160–161
  attack on, 163
  origins of, 161–162
Haroon, Mohammed, 92
Hassan, Mullah, 102
  escape of, 106
Hazara, 14
Hekmatyar, Gulbuddin, 10
  bin Laden and, 17
  Charasyab and, 12
  Dostum and, 14, 16–17
  Jamaat-e-Islami and, 158
  Pakistan and, 41
  training of, 139
Herat, 43
Heroin, 55
Hezb-e-Islami, 5
  Hekmatyar and, 10
Hezb-e-Wahadat, 71
Hezb-ul Mujahedeen, 160–161
Hindus, 128
Holl, Norbert, 48
Hospitals, in Kabul, 15–16
Hostages, 151–154
Hussein, Saddam, 172

Imam, Pakistani colonel, 41
India
  Kashmir and, 38
  Muslims in, 128
  nuclear weapons and, 134–135
  Pakistan and, 127
International Relief Agency, 101
Iran
  Beg, Mirza Aslam, and, 144
  CENTO and, 132
  nuclear weapons and, 145
  SEATO and, 131

Stinger missiles and, 7
Taliban and, 76–77
Iraq, 131
ISI (Inter-Services Intelligence), 40
  Ahmed and, 92–93
  CIA and, 140
  Gul and, 138, 143
  Hakim and, 154
  militant Muslims and, 157
  Nasir and, 159
  recruitment, 42
Islam
  banking, 141–142
  Bhutto, Zulfikar Ali, and, 135, 138
  conservative, 136
  Jamaat-e-Islami and, 159
  in Morocco, 170
  Omar and, 41
  in Pakistan, 130, 147
  perception of, 172
  1970s revival of, 136
  Taliban and, 33, 86–87
  Wahabi, 33
Islami Jamiat-e-Tulaba, 160
Islamic Medical Association, 160
Israel, 172

Jabbar, Abdul, 90
Jacobsen, Sally, 85
Jaish-e-Mohammed, 77, 161
Jaish-e-Muslimeen, 150, 152
Jamaah Islamiya, 142
Jamaat, Tableeqi, 137
Jamaat-e-Islami, 138
  adherents, 158
  education and, 160
  ideology, 158–159
  structure of, 159–160
Jamal, Qadratullah, 97, 102, 110
  escape of, 106
Jamiat-e-Ulema Islam, 138
Jammu-Kashmir Liberation Front,
  161
Jan, Abdul, 110–111
Jan, Ghulam, 14
Jan, Hajji, 22, 23
Jandal, Abu, 167–173
Jehangir, Asma, 147–148

Jihad, 147
    Jamaat-e-Islami and, 159
    al Qaeda and, 171
Jihadis, 38
    groups, 160–161
    Pakistan and, 155
Jinnah, Mohammed Ali, 128
Jirga, 29–30, 130
Jamaat-e-Islami, 157
Junejo, Mohammed Khan, 142

Kabul
    attack on, 90
    evacuation of, 90–91
    hospitals, 15–16
    land mines in, 16
    mujahedeen and, 1, 9–10, 18
    Northern Alliance and, 104
    Taliban withdrawal from, 106–107
Kabul University, 8
Kabul Zoo, 12–13
Kandahar, 29
    Arabs in, 32
    bin Laden in, 76
    history of, 33–34
    Taliban takeover of, 47
    Taliban withdrawal from, 110
Karamat, Jehangir, 145
Karim, Fazl, 101, 149–151
Karimov, Islam, 67
Karzai, Hamid
    Abdullah and, 2
    election of, 154
    Pakistan and, 58
    Sherzai and, 29
    on Taliban, 57–58
    Taliban and, 110
Kashmir, 38, 128
    election in, 161–162
Khaksar, Mullah Mohammed, 21, 161
    on Amir-ul Momineen, 44
    CIA and, 62–65
    Massood and, 65
    McIllwain and, 63–64
    Omar and, 25
    Pakistani mullahs and, 39
    Shah, Amir, and, 22–24
    Taliban and, 24–25, 27

    on UN, 54
    United States and, 61–62
Khalid bin Walid, 163
Khalil, Fazlur Rahman, 161
Khalilzad, Zalmay, 113–114
Khalis, Maulvi Younis, 5, 35
    on education of women, 49
    Harakat-ul Mujahedeen and, 161
Khan, A. Q., 136, 145
Khan, Aziz, 71
Khan, Darya, 124
Khan, Ghulam Ishaq, 144
Khan, Zarwar, 117
Khorazon, 155
Khudaidad, Mullah, 43
    strength of, 57
Koochi, Naeem, 116
Kosovo, 166

Land mines, 5–6, 16
Latif, Mansour, 110
Libya, 136

M–11 missiles, 145
Macroyan, 14–15
Madrassas, 147
Mai, Muktarai, 148
Maidan Shahr, 48
Malik, Abdul, 68–69
    ambush by, 71–72
Marchese, Gregory, 63
Marjan, Wali, 115
Massood, Ahmed Shah, 2, 10
    assassination of, 83
    Khaksar and, 65
    training of, 139
Maswak, 156
Mazar-e-Sharif, 67
    Northern Alliance in, 95
    Taliban in, 69–70, 75
    United Nations and, 75
McIllwain, Peter, 62
    Khaksar and, 63–64
Mecca, 9
    Ahmedis and, 136
Mercer, Heather, 84, 107–108
Mercer, John, 86, 91
Messinis, Dimitri, 97

Minefields. *See* Land mines
Mohammed, Abdul, 116
Mohammed, Khalid Sheikh, 158
Mohammed, Sufi, 96
Momin, General, 53
Morocco, 170
Muawyia, 163
Mujahedeen
    booby-traps, 16
    corruption in, 27–28
    Kabul and, 1, 9–10
    Sevan, Benon, and, 53–54
    United States and, 140
    withdrawal in Kabul of, 18
    al-Zawahri and, 75
Mullahs, 38–40
Musharraf, Pervez, 93
    in Afghanistan, 154
    appointment of, 145
    assassination attempt on, 162
    Bush and, 146
    Clinton and, 145–146
    history of, 162–163
    Jehangir and, 148
    9/11 attacks and, 146
    United States and, 133
Music, 111–112
    Taliban and, 33
Muslims, 128
    militant, 157
    revenge and, 169
    Shiite, 72
    torture of, 172
Muttawakil, Wakil Ahmed, 56
    on 9/11 attack, 87–88

Nagma, 33
Najibullah, 4, 156
    body of, 51
    downfall of, 7–9
    murder of, 19
    UN and, 9, 52–53
Namangani, Juman, 76
Napalm bombs, 5
Nasir, Javed, 159
National Labor Federation, 160
Niazi, Amir Abdullah Khan, 133
9/11 attacks, 58, 83–86

Masharraf and, 146
Muttawakil on, 87–88
Nodong missiles, 145
North American Treaty Organization
    (NATO), 131
North Korea, 145, 172
Northern Alliance
    attack on Kabul, 90
    bin Laden and, 32
    dominance of, 1
    Kabul and, 104
    in Mazar-e-Sharif, 95
    reduction of, 55
    United States and, 94–95, 113
Nuclear weapons, 134–135
    China and, 145
    development, 136
    Iran and, 145
    sanctions and, 142, 143

Obeidullah, Defense Minister, 79
Oddy, Deborah, 86
Omar, Mohammed, 83
Omar, Mullah
    Ahmed and, 93–94
    al Qaeda and, 92–93
    Amir-ul Momineen and, 44–45
    bin Laden and, 31–32, 93
    computers and, 86
    corruption and, 28–29
    fear of, 57
    history of, 25
    Islamic devotion of, 41
    Khaksar and, 21–22, 25
    leadership of, 30
    Pakistan and, 164
    Pakistani mullahs and, 39–40
    paranoia of, 77
    Quran and, 37–38
    recruitment efforts by, 75
    Sharia and, 40
Operation Anaconda, 110
Operation Enduring Freedom, 94
Opium, 59–60

Pahlawan, Abdur Rahman, 68
Pakistan
    Afghanistan and, 92

Pakistan *(cont.)*
  alcohol in, 138
  banking in, 141–142
  education in, 147
  Hekmatyar and, 41
  history óf, 127–147
  Islam in, 147
  Jihadis and, 155
  Karzai and, 58
  Kashmir and, 38
  military takeover of, 93
  mullahs, 38–40
  nuclear weapons and, 135, 136
  Omar and, 164
  sanctions against, 142, 143
  socialism in, 135
  withdrawal from SEATO, 135
Pakistan Business Forum, 160
Pakistan Military Academy, 136
Pakistan National Alliance, 137–138
Panjshir Valley, 83, 125
Pashtuns
  alienation of, 113
  allies of, 41
  in Pakistan, 128
  Taliban and, 23
  traditions, 74
  treatment of, 118–119, 124
Pentagon, 85
Philippines, 142
Photography, 34
  banning of, 26
  video, 96
Pirs, 33
Poppies, 55
  ban on, 60–61
  history of, 59–60
Pressler, Larry, 142
Prison. *See also* Guantanamo
  in Bagram, 121–122
  mistreatment, 121–123
  Pul-e-Charkhi, 23
  in Shebergan, 120
  United States, 121
Proselytizing, 84
Pul-e-Charkhi, 3
  prison, 23
Punjab, 128

al Qaeda
  education and, 147
  finances, 157–158
  financing by, 77
  Jihad and, 171
  Jamaat-e-Islami and, 157
  Omar and, 92–93
  organization of, 87
  perspective of, 169
  recruitment for, 73
Qali-e-Jhangi, 68
Qayyam, 121–122
Quran
  Guantanamo and, 120–121
  Haq, Zia-ul, and, 137
  Omar and, 37–38
  paper and, 86–87
  on women's rights, 49

Rabbani, Burhanuddin, 18
  UN and, 54
Radio Shariat, 89
Rahman, Abdur, 169
Rahman, Saif-ur, 110, 121–122
Rape
  Dostum and, 68
  Hadood Ordinance and, 141
  in Hazara, 14
  of Mai, 148
Rawalpindi, 94
Razzak, Abdul, 107
Reagan, Ronald, 4, 139
  on communism, 8
  Haq, Zia-ul, and, 141
Red Army, 5
Red Cross, 1–2
Rishkore, 76
Roads, 28
Royal Military Academy, 131
Rumsfeld, Donald, 114

Sadat, Anwar, 75
Sahab, Hajji, 103, 107
Saifullah, Qari, 162
Saleh, Commander, 30–31
Sam–7 missile, 6
Sanctions, 77, 79
Sandhurst, 131

Sanghisar, 25, 28, 31
Sanghir, Mohammed, 120
Saquo, Bacha, 46
Saudi Arabia, 136
Sayyaf, Abdul Rasul, 10
  Afghan Interior Ministry and,
    11–12
  alliances of, 161
  atrocities of, 54
  bin Laden and, 32
  criticism of, 123
  Jamaat-e-Islami and, 158
  Pakistani support for, 142
  Shah, Amir, and, 104
  United States and, 166
SEATO. *See* Southeast Asia Treaty
    Organization
Services Center, 141
Sevan, Benon, 53–54
Shabab-e-Milli, 159
Shah, Amir, 11
  in Bamiyan, 80–81
  burqas and, 48
  on Dasht-e-Barchi, 13
  Khaksar and, 22–24
  Sayyaf and, 104
Shah, Habiba, 48
Shalwar kameez, 24, 37
Shamzai, Nizamuddin, 39
Sharia, 35
  Omar and, 40
Sharif, Nawaz, 144
Shaukat, Saifullah, 161
Shebergan, 68
  prison in, 120
Sherzai, Gul Aga, 29
Shrine of the Cloak of the Prophet, 33
Shura, 29
Socialism, 135
Somali, Haza, 169
Southeast Asia Treaty Organization
    (SEATO), 131
  Pakistan's withdrawal from, 135
Soviet Union, 4
  CENTO and, 132
  invasion of Afghanistan, 139
  withdrawal of, 7
Srinagar, 130

Stanikzai, Sher Mohammed, 107
Statues, destruction of, 78–81
Stinger missiles, 7
Students, recruitment of, 38–39
Suicide bombers, 155–156, 167
Surmad, 109–110

Tableequi, 120
Tajuddin, 125
Taliban
  ambush of, 71–72
  ascendance of, 9
  BBC and, 105
  bin Laden and, 163
  CIA and, 32
  Dostum and, 67–68
  external influence on, 63–64
  financing of, 77
  Hakim and, 152
  heroin and, 55
  Iran and, 76–77
  ISI and, 40
  Islam and, 33
  in Kabul, 1
  Karzai and, 57–58, 110
  Khaksar and, 24–25, 27
  Malik and, 68–69
  in Mazar-e-Sharif, 69–70
  moderates of, 56
  music and, 33
  Najibullah and, 19
  origins of, 27–31
  Pakistani control of, 42
  Pashtu and, 23
  radical Islamists v., 86–87
  recruitment, 38
  retaliation in Mazar-e-Sharif, 75
  Shiite Muslims and, 72
  slaughter of, 72
  takeover of Kandahar, 47
  trials of, 74
  UN and, 54
  Western perception of, 47
  withdrawal from Kabul, 106–107
  withdrawal from Kandahar, 110
Technology, 86–87
Terrorism, 85
  bin Laden and, 85

Terrorism *(cont.)*
   training camps, 170
   U.S. war on, 122, 157
Theft, 28
Torture
   of Muslims, 172
   in Pul-e-Charkhi, 23
Turkey, 131, 132

Uighurs, 39, 159
United Nations (UN)
   evacuation of Kabul, 90–91
   guest house, 4
   hostages, 153–154
   Jehangir and, 148
   Khaksar on, 54
   Mazar-e-Sharif and, 75
   Najibullah and, 9, 52–53
   Rabbani and, 54
   sanctions by, 77, 79
   Sevan and, 53
   Taliban and, 47, 54
   women's rights and, 48, 55
United States, 4–5
   alliances of, 166
   army, 118
   attack on bin Laden, 75
   bombing by, 107
   CENTO and, 132
   Haq, Zia-ul, and, 139
   Khaksar and, 61–62
   Masharraf and, 133
   mujahedeen and, 140
   Northern Alliance and, 94–95, 113
   Pakistan and, 127

   prisons, 120–121
   propaganda, 141
   Seventh Fleet, 133
   training camps, 139
   troops, 112–113
   war on terror, 122, 157
US Commander and Staff College, 137
USS Cole, 85
Uzbekistan, 67

Wahabis, 41
Wakil, Hajji Ruhollah, 121
Wazeer, Mullah, 116
Wazir Akbar Khan Hospital, 99, 101
Weapons dealing, 29
Wild, Roland, 46
Women
   education and, 49
   Jamaat-e-Islami and, 159
   treatment of, 47–48
Women's rights
   Quran on, 49
   UN and, 48, 55
World Trade Center, 85

Yousuf, General, 69

Zabul Province, 118–119
Zadran, Bacha Khan, 115
Zakat, 141
Zareen, Malik, 122
al-Zawahri, Aymen, 5, 95
   mujahedeen and, 75
   Sayyaf and, 161
Zubdayda, Abu, 157–158

PublicAffairs is a publishing house founded in 1997. It is a tribute to the standards, values, and flair of three persons who have served as mentors to countless reporters, writers, editors, and book people of all kinds, including me.

I. F. Stone, proprietor of *I. F. Stone's Weekly,* combined a commitment to the First Amendment with entrepreneurial zeal and reporting skill and became one of the great independent journalists in American history. At the age of eighty, Izzy published *The Trial of Socrates,* which was a national bestseller. He wrote the book after he taught himself ancient Greek.

Benjamin C. Bradlee was for nearly thirty years the charismatic editorial leader of *The Washington Post.* It was Ben who gave the *Post* the range and courage to pursue such historic issues as Watergate. He supported his reporters with a tenacity that made them fearless, and it is no accident that so many became authors of influential, best-selling books.

Robert L. Bernstein, the chief executive of Random House for more than a quarter century, guided one of the nation's premier publishing houses. Bob was personally responsible for many books of political dissent and argument that challenged tyranny around the globe. He is also the founder and was the longtime chair of Human Rights Watch, one of the most respected human rights organizations in the world.

．　　　．　　　．

For fifty years, the banner of Public Affairs Press was carried by its owner Morris B. Schnapper, who published Gandhi, Nasser, Toynbee, Truman, and about 1,500 other authors. In 1983 Schnapper was described by *The Washington Post* as "a redoubtable gadfly." His legacy will endure in the books to come.

Peter Osnos, *Publisher*